ISLAM
Religion, Practice, Culture and World Order

ISLAM
Religion, Practice, Culture and World Order

ISMAʿĪL R. AL FĀRŪQĪ

with an Introduction by
Imtiyaz Yusuf

THE INTERNATIONAL INSTITUTE OF ISLAMIC THOUGHT
LONDON • WASHINGTON

THE INTERNATIONAL INSTITUTE OF ISLAMIC THOUGHT
P.O. BOX 669, HERNDON, VA 20172, USA
www.iiit.org

LONDON OFFICE
P.O. BOX 126, RICHMOND, SURREY TW9 2UD, UK
www.iiituk.com

ISBN 978-1-56564-587-5 *limp*
ISBN 978-1-56564-588-2 *cased*

Typesetting by Sideek Ali
Cover design by Shiraz Khan

Contents

Foreword

Genuine understanding of Islam, the religion, will reveal ... that Islam is a later moment of that very consciousness which produced Judaism and Christianity; that Islam, the culture, is as much a source of the Western civilization of the present millennium as classical Greece and Rome ... that Islam's anti-clericalism made it the first "Protestant" revolution, that its rationalism made it the first "Enlightenment," that its pragmatism made it the first "technocracy," and that its law of war and peace made it the first "United Nations."

So writes Professor Isma'īl Rājī al Fārūqī, Palestinian-American philosopher, visionary, an authority in comparative religion and one of the great Muslim scholars of the 20th century. In this study al Fārūqī presents the meaning and message of Islam to the wider world community. Key elements of the faith are summarised and explained in an overall theme of seven parts consisting of 21 chapters in total. Yet the chapters represent far more than a simple description of Muslim peoples and orthodox practice. Al Fārūqī was a great thinker and relished intellectual engagement on every level, particularly when it came to Islam and other Faiths. And it is this unique reasoning process that is reflected in this work, al Fārūqī's signature contribution, which not only expounds on Islam as spiritual faith and action, but also on Islam *the great experience.*

Murdered in 1986 the legacy of his thought and action continue to inform and impress the discourse on Islam, Islamic reform and its institutions throughout the world. Al Fārūqī also laid the foundation for a new interpretation and analysis of *tawḥīd* (the unity of God) and its relevance to knowledge, life, and thought. His rigorously intellectual approach and formidable logic raised the standard of Islamic scholarship to new and higher levels. Al Fārūqī played a central and ideational role in devising a model for a contemporary Islamic university, making intellectual contributions to curriculum development and designing the research programmes of Islamic universities in several countries. Al Fārūqī also broke new grounds in establishing university-level Islamic studies programs in the West. He was, and remains, a brilliant intellectual, whose remarkable legacy of reform and scholastic efforts still resonate today.

This work is the resurrection of a manuscript completed in the mid-seventies by al Fārūqī, exploring and explaining the many key dimensions that make up the Islamic faith. Aside from minor typos the work has been largely left unrevised and unedited, faithful to the author's original rendering. In addition, chapter headings have been retained as originally composed. No doubt there is a need to 'know' Islam as never before, and this book – timely as the day it was written – attempts to generate this complete understanding. As al Fārūqī remarks in his Preface, readers are invited, in a spirit of "fellowship", to enter the world of Islam and become familiar with its integral components and the way it is lived on a daily basis.

Where dates are cited according to the Islamic calendar (hijrah) they are labelled AH. Otherwise they follow the Gregorian calendar and labelled CE where necessary. Arabic words are italicized except for those which have entered common usage. Diacritical marks have been added only to those Arabic names not considered contemporary. The exception being al Fārūqī, whose name has been written according to his own preference.

The IIIT, established in 1981, has served as a major center to facilitate serious scholarly efforts based on Islamic vision, values and principles. The Institute's programs of research, seminars and conferences during the last thirty years have resulted in the publication of more than four hundred titles both in English, Arabic and other major languages.

IIIT LONDON OFFICE
SEPTEMBER 2012

BRIEF BIOGRAPHY OF
Isma'īl Rājī al Fārūqī
(1921–1986)

PROFESSOR Isma'īl Rājī al Fārūqī was born in Jaffa, Palestine. He was a great contemporary scholar of Islam and his scholarship encompassed the whole spectrum of Islamic Studies covering areas such as the study of religion, Islamic thought, approaches to knowledge, history, culture, education, interfaith dialogue, aesthetics, ethics, politics, economics, science and women's issues. It is no exaggeration to say that his was indeed a remarkably encyclopedic mind, and that he himself was a rare personality among contemporary Muslim scholars.

Al Fārūqī at first emigrated to Beirut, Lebanon, where he studied at the American University of Beirut, enrolling the following year at Indiana University's Graduate School of Arts and Sciences, to obtain an M.A. in philosophy in 1949. He was then accepted for entry into Harvard University's department of philosophy where he was awarded a second M.A. in philosophy in March 1951. However, he decided to return to Indiana University where he submitted his Ph.D thesis to the department of philosophy obtaining his doctorate in September 1952. The title of his thesis was, "Justifying the Good: Metaphysics and Epistemology of Value".

Al Fārūqī then studied Islam in Cairo and other centers of Muslim learning, and Christianity at the Faculty of Divinity, McGill University. He taught at the Institute of Islamic Studies, McGill University; the Central Institute of Islamic Research, Karachi; the Institute of Higher Arabic Studies of the League of Arab States, Cairo University; Al-Azhar University, Cairo; and at Syracuse University, USA, where he held the position of Associate Professor of Religion between 1964 and 1968, developing a program of Islamic Studies.

In the Fall of 1968 Al Fārūqī became professor of Islamic studies and history of religions in the Department of Religion, Temple University, a position he held until his tragic death in 1986.

Introduction

But do not think of those that have been slain in God's cause as dead. Nay, they are alive! With their Sustainer have they their sustenance. (Qur'an 3:169)

For, they who have attained to faith in God and His Apostle – it is they, they who uphold the truth, and they who bear witness [thereto] before God: [and so] they shall have their reward and their light! But as for those who are bent on denying the truth and on giving the lie to Our messages – it is they who are destined for the blazing fire! (Qur'an 57:19)

PROFESSOR Isma'īl Rājī al Fārūqī was a trailblazer of Islamics or Islamic Studies in the modern age. Since the 1960s onwards, al Fārūqī, along with Professor Fazlur Rahman of the University of Chicago and Professor Seyyed Hossein Nasr of George Washington University, were the most prominent scholars of Islamics in north America, when Islamics was making an appearance as a discipline of study, research and discourse at the universities. Each of them made their special contributions – Fazlur Rahman in Islamic thought, Seyyed Hossein Nasr in Islamic mysticism and Isma'īl al Fārūqī in the study of Islam within the academic study of religion and Islamization of Knowledge.

Al Fārūqī wrote several books and chapters of introduction to Islam viz., chapters on Islam in Wing T. Chan, (ed.) *Great Asian Religions: An Anthology,* (Macmillan, 1969); and also in his own book *Historical Atlas of the Religions of the World* (Macmillan, 1975) which he co-edited with David E. Sopher. He also wrote a lengthy introduction to Islam in a book titled, *Islam* (Argus Communications, 1979, current editions published by Amana Publications) and Isma'īl al Fārūqī, *The Cultural Atlas of Islam,* (Macmillan, 1986) published posthumously.

I discovered the manuscript of this book "Introduction to Islam" as a finished work in Isma'īl al Fārūqī's papers at the International Institute of Islamic Thought, (IIIT) Herndon, VA, USA in 2010.

Introduction

In the years, 2009-2010, I was appointed as a visiting associate professor and the Malaysia Chair for Islam in Southeast Asia at the Alwaleed bin Talal Center for Muslim-Christian Understanding, Georgetown University, Washington D.C., USA. This appointment came as a God given opportunity to fulfill my dream of contributing towards making the scholarship and memory of al Fārūqī a continuing legacy for our and future generations. I was glad to be given the opportunity to access the Fārūqī papers at the IIIT. I remain grateful to Dr. Jamal Barzinji, Dr. Hisham Altalib, Dr. Iqbal Unus and Dr. Abu Baker al-Shingieti for giving me access and for trusting in my ambition to contribute towards making al Fārūqī's contribution a living heritage. I went through the Fārūqī papers covering his academic career between the years 1961 and 1986, which gave me a unique insight into the personality, mind and contributions of one of the great scholars of Islam. These papers are a mine of resources, containing al Fārūqī's published and unpublished works and activities covering various topics and areas of knowledge, thought, and research in the life of a Muslim intellectual. It would take a lifetime to work on them as a field of research. I have decided to work only on published and unpublished works of al Fārūqī in the area of study of religion and Islam, which is the area of my academic research interest. *Inshā'Allāh*, I hope to complete this during my lifetime.

My association with Ismaᶜīl al Fārūqī began in 1984 when he offered me a scholarship to pursue my doctoral studies at the Department of Religion, Temple University, Philadelphia, USA. I was fortunate to study with al Fārūqī courses such as Ancient Near Texts, Qur'an, Islam and Art, Introduction to Muslim and Christian Theology through the Study of Abul Ala Maududi and Karl Barth, and History of Religions. From the deep knowledge we received from al Fārūqī, and his insistence that we pursue high standards of academic study and research with rigorous methodology, we – his students – were forged to perform up to his high expectations and pursue a high standard of scholarship. For us, he was a walking encyclopedia, full of intellectual energy, academic enthusiasm, and a great scholar with deep knowledge of Islam and world religions – a rare combination of intellect and accomplishment by a contemporary Muslim scholar.

Introduction

Al Fārūqī probably finished writing this manuscript in 1975. Why 1975? In the original dated manuscript which I have now updated, al Fārūqī mentions in chapter 9, titled Hajj, that Muslims have performed the Hajj 1395 times until 1975. Hence my conclusion that this manuscript was written in 1975.

In spite of being a 36 years old manuscript, the contents of this book are as fresh as ever. I have not changed its main theme or contents except for some corrections following the remarks al Fārūqī had made on the sidelines of the manuscript, which he did not incorporate. I have updated the statistical information contained in the manuscript, bringing them up to date to current times.

This insider introduction to Islam is written by al Fārūqī within the parameters of his methodological approach to the study of Islam and religion. Al Fārūqī's approach to the study and presentation of Islam is based on three methods viz., history of religion and the phenomenological approach towards Islam combined with a Fārūqīan view of interreligious dialogue from an Islamic perspective.

Employing the history of religions approach from a Muslim perspective based on the study and knowledge of historical critical research of Ancient Near Eastern history and text, al Fārūqī proposes a non-nationalistic view of ʿurūbah – Arabism as a monotheistic worldview and source of Muslim civilization. For al Fārūqī, the Arabs are the founders of monotheism in the history of religions and the monotheistic conception of dīn. This had appeared in the form of Arab religious humanism expressed in the Jewish, Christian and Muslim forms of monotheism, i.e. religion in the Arab mind.

ʿUrūbah is an integral part of Arab consciousness; it is an Arab view of the world formed on the basis of a monotheistic view of religion. The emergence of monotheism through poetic reflections and religious meditation of Arab ḥanīfs – monotheists and prophets – transformed the Arabs from a tribal culture to a world religious community. Monotheism integrated the Arabs.

Al Fārūqī commented that all Arabs are monotheists, "All those who have inhabited the Near East, whether permanently or transiently, were Arabs. All of them have contributed to the legacy which the

Arabs proudly call their own."[1] As per al Fārūqī, the Arabs have been the carriers of the divine message of monotheism in the history of religion.

Using an innovative and modern scholarly approach toward the study of Islam and its civilization, al Fārūqī addressed the concept of *dīn* identified with the theology of *tawḥīd* – unity of God both historically and ideationally. This is evidenced in al Fārūqī's early works such as *ʿUrūbah and Religion* where he asserted that *ʿurūbah* when interpreted in its non-Arab nationalist notion contains the core of Muslim religious consciousness, its faith and its values. And this has been recognized by both the Arabs and non-Arabs who became the members of the monotheistic religions of Judaism, Christianity and Islam. This approach to Islamic religion and civilization is al Fārūqī's academically solid foundational approach to Islam which reverberates again and again in this book. This Fārūqian non-nationalistic view of Islam should not unnerve the non-Arab Muslims, who through their histor-ical encounter, cultural experience and religious creativity imbibed the Arab view of *dīn* based on *tawḥīd* – monotheism – in their various geographic environments, thereby contributing towards the flower-ing of Islam as a worldwide universal civilization. In fact, as a universal religion Islam asserts that *tawḥīd* as belief in One, Universal God is not the sole property of a geographic community such as the Arabs. It does not belong to the Arab in a nationalistic or racist sense. God bequeathed the notion of *tawḥīd* to the Arabs as a part of humanity since pre-historic times and they shared it with the rest of humanity with the emergence of Islam. Before the Muslims, Judaism and Christianity too contained the concept of monotheism but the Jews made it exclusive to themselves turning monotheism into a nationalis-tic ideology. And the Christians split over defining monotheism as seen through the Christological debates engaged in by the ante-Nicene and post-Nicene Fathers[2] as well as Arabian and Western Christianity.[3]

---

1 Isma'il al-Faruqi, *'Urubah and Religion* (Amsterdam: Djambatan, 1962), p. 9.

2 Alexander Roberts et al., *The Ante-Nicene Fathers*. 10 volumes (Hendrickson Publishers, 1994). Alexander Roberts et al., *Nicene and Post-Nicene Fathers*. 14 volumes (Hendrickson Publishers, 1994). W. H. C. Frend, *Rise of Christianity* (Fortress Press, 1986).

3 Isma'il al-Faruqi, *'Urubah and Religion*, p. 101.

Introduction

Adopting the phenomenological approach towards Islam, al Fārūqī presents knowledge about Islam as it appears to the consciousness without bracketing it through Muslim cultural prejudices and biases. In this sense, al Fārūqī was the foremost Muslim phenomenologist of religion of the modern age, following in the earlier Muslim tradition of phenomenology of religion evidenced in the works of al-Bayrūnī (973-1048) and Ibn Ḥazm (994-1064) whose works he admired tremendously.

Al Fārūqī was a pioneer and active participant in Islam's dialogue with other religions in the West. As a citizen and resident in the West, al Fārūqī engaged actively in the interreligious dialogue movement which in the 1960s was in its early stages in the West, following the dialogue initiatives of the World Council of Churches and the II Vatican Council. In this book one feels the presence of the dialogical aspect of al Fārūqī's intellectual engagement as he presents the meaning and message of Islam to the wider world community. In this endeavor he adapts Muslim epistemology to changing times.

Al Fārūqī laid the foundation for a new interpretation and analysis of the quintessence of the Islamic religious principle of *tawḥīd* and its relevance to different dimensions of human life, thought and practice. In fact, his various academic contributions raised the level of Islamic scholarship to a new higher intellectual stage whose relevance continues until today.

Al Fārūqī has left behind a school of thought known as the school of Islamization of knowledge which operates at the level of university education at several Islamic universities around the globe. His school of thought, academic approach and practice is also being applied by hundreds of his students teaching and doing research at different universities around the globe.

As a former student of al Fārūqī, whose inspiration continues to shape my personal and academic life, I dedicate my effort in editing and updating this book to my teacher and mentor. Indeed, I have felt al Fārūqī's presence beside me during the process of working on the manuscript.

Introduction

May Allah (SWT)* bless Professor al Fārūqī and his wife Dr. Lois Lamya al Fārūqī (1926-1986), whose lives and tragic deaths have become a part of our memory, everyday life, thought and practice. I will always remain their student.

IMTIYAZ YUSUF
PROFESSOR OF ISLAMICS AND RELIGION
*Graduate School of Philosophy and Religion,
Assumption University Bangkok, Thailand*

MARCH 2011

---

*(SWT) – *Subḥānahu wa Taʿālā*: May He be praised and may His transcendence be affirmed. Said when referring to God.

Preface

WHEN ISLAM AROSE in the seventh century CE, it spread across continents with shocking speed. Its political power eclipsed and brought down the two formidable empires of the world, Persia and Byzantium. The convincing logic of its theological claim, the ennobling uplift of its pietism and morality, the pragmatic efficiency of its law, the appealing universality of its brotherhood, and the moving commitment and liberality of its adherents – all these disarmed the millions and persuaded them to join its ranks. For a thousand years it was unparalleled in its world power, affluence, high civilization and culture. For a thousand years it was the only challenger of Europe, and it came close to a conquest of that continent. Europe put up a fight with it in a dozen crusades, all of which came to naught. Another campaign launched by Christendom in Spain succeeded and brought to an end seven centuries of Islamic dominion in the Iberian Peninsula. It was only in modern times, i.e., in the last two centuries, that Europe succeeded in conquering the Muslim World, and subjecting it to colonial fragmentation and rule. Even then, the religion of Islam continued to spread in Asia and Africa, and to do so at a greater pace than Christianity, despite the support its missionaries received from the colonial power.

This long history of confrontation and conflict gave rise to countless rumors and fabrications designed to place Islam and its adherents in a bad light. Together with misunderstandings of a religion and culture that are different from one's own, the antagonistic allegations became built-in prejudices, hard to shake off. A very special care is therefore needed by the student of Islam to remain open minded, and a very special effort is called for to empathize with the data, if he is to understand them as they are.

The reward for such exertion is great. Genuine understanding of Islam, the religion, will reveal to the student that Islam is a later moment of that very consciousness which produced Judaism and Christianity; that Islam, the culture, is as much a source of the Western civilization of the present millennium as classical Greece and Rome. He will discover that Islam's anti-clericalism made it the first "Protestant" revolution, that its rationalism made it the first "Enlightenment," that its pragmatism made it the first "technocracy," and that its law of war and peace made it the first "United Nations."

Once this vision is achieved, it becomes easy to relate oneself to the sixth of humanity in understanding and fellowship. That is what you are here invited to achieve.

Temple University
Isma'īl Rājī al Fārūqī
Philadelphia, Pennsylvania

C. 1975

Part I

CHAPTER I

Who is a Muslim?

OUT of a world population of 6.9 billion, 1.3 billion are Muslims. Both these figures are approximate since no exact statistics are available. They are, however, reasonable since the former is based on United Nations assessments, and the latter on the calculations by each country of its Muslim population. Every sixth man, woman, and child on earth, therefore, is a Muslim.

Muslims constitute the majorities of the fifty seven members of the Organization of Islamic Conference. They constitute significant minorities in a number of other countries: India (161 million), China (22 million), Russia (16 million), as well as lesser minorities in practically every country in the world.

In North America, Muslims count about eight million persons, most of whom live in the big cities. New York, Chicago, Detroit, Toronto, Montreal, Los Angeles, Philadelphia, Washington and Boston are home to thousands of Muslims. Many an American town has a number of mosques (Arabic: *masjid*, pl. *masājid*) or houses of prayer, where Muslims worship. The largest and most beautiful of these is the Mosque of Washington, D.C. located on Massachusetts Avenue. It was completed in 1957 under the patronage of a number of Muslim Governments. 6,000 worshipers attend Friday prayer there every week.

Who is a Muslim?

The Muslims belong to practically all world ethnic groups. The Arabs, as ethnic group, lead the list with some 316 million, followed by the Javanese (239 million), Bengalis (147 million), and the Turanians, i.e., Turkmen in Central Asia and Asia Minor (61 million). Although black people constitute an ethnic group in America, they do not do so in the world where they are divided into a number of properly "ethnic" groupings. Nonetheless, there are 241 million Muslims of African descent.

The map of the Muslim World looks like a solid rectangle running over the great land mass of Africa-Asia. It stretches from Dakar, the westernmost corner of Africa all the way to Sinkiang in northwest China. The "rectangle" seems also to have three long and heavy fingers stretched over the east coast of Africa, a second along the great river plains of northern India and reaching to the Bay of Bengal, and a third, stretching over the whole archipelago of the East Indies and including part of the Philippines and New Guinea. By area, the Muslim World includes two of the largest countries in the world, Kazakhastan and Sudan. By population, it includes four of the most populous, namely, Indonesia, Pakistan, Bangladesh and Nigeria with a combined population of over 600 million.

Muslims speak many languages. Those of them for whom Arabic is the mother-tongue make up over 316 million. The Javanese group is next in size and counts some 239 million; the Bengali, 147 million; the Turkish 70 million; the Persian, 69 million and the Hausa groups, 35 million respectively. Arabic is also a *lingua franca* to many more millions of non-Arabic speaking peoples. All Muslims know some measure of Arabic, since Arabic is the language of worship. Many have achieved varying degrees of mastery of the language since it is the first language of Islamic religious thought and culture. A person speaking and writing nothing but Arabic could easily find himself at home anywhere around the wider world belt, Dakar to Mindanao, among Muslim communities.

A very prominent and visible aspect of universal occurrence among Muslims consists in Arabic calligraphy and arabesque decoration, found in all places where Muslims congregate, especially in the houses of worship. Equally ubiquitous are various architectural features of those buildings, whether inside, as in the case of the Qur'an's verses rendered in beautiful calligraphy, or outside, such as the minarets, from which five times a day, the *muadhdhin* chants the call to worship in Arabic. This call to prayer, as well as the chanting of the Qur'an, constitutes aural features of universal occurrence in the Muslim World. Certainly, there are other features binding the Muslim World together, but they are not as conspicuous. They reveal themselves to the investigator, if not to the casual tourist.

Besides these foregoing aspects of quick identification, Muslims constitute a great diversity of appearances. They are divided into a multiplicity of cultural groups, each carrying its own dress, customs, and ways of life.

In the past, the Muslim World has witnessed a great deal of mobility among its peoples. The brotherhood, racial tolerance and lack of color discrimination, the common institutions of the Muslims, once made it possible for anyone to move from one end of the empire to another without estrangement. As a direct effect of this mobility, the Muslim urban populations are very polyglot. No feast is greater to the eyes of the anthropologist than that of sitting at any sidewalk cafe in Rabat, Tripoli, Cairo, Damascus, Jeddah, Baghdad, Tehran, Lahore, Delhi, or Jakarta. Passing him are automobiles as well as camels, veiled women as well as women in saris and mini-skirts, jeans and sarongs, fair and blue-eyed northerners as well as people of dark skin, West African Hamitic, Chinese or Mongols, small-built Malays or large bodied Afghans, men with parted hair and men with fezzes, and turbans, men in Savile Row clothing and men in flowing robes. All of them are Muslims.

The same diversity is beginning to characterize Muslim presence in North America. Whereas half of the Muslims of this continent are black people, the other half are caucasian, and consist of immigrants (and their descendants) from all over the Muslim World. The same variety of ethnic and cultural types can be witnessed in any convention of the Islamic Society of North America (ISNA), the dominant and guiding Muslim organization in the North American continent.

CHAPTER 2

What is a Muslim?

EVERY law court of Islam is bound to recognize as a Muslim in good standing, and hence as entitled to all privileges and rights appertaining thereto, and standing under all duties and obligations of Islamic law, every adult male and female who consciously and solemnly witnesses that "There is no God but God and Muhammad is the Prophet of God." Fulfillment of this simple definition of "Islamicity" is all that Islamic law requires in order to ascertain membership in the Muslim community. Once a person is put to the test, and he witnesses responsibly to the twin facts of God being the only God and Muhammad (ṢAAS)* being His Prophet, no more can be legally required of him to prove his faith and, in consequence, all his rights and duties under Islamic law.

The reason why "Islamicity" is so simple to define, so simple to attain and so simple to establish, is that Islam is neither an ethnocentric nor a sacramental religion. One does not have to be born a Muslim; nor does one have to have any Muslim parent, guardian, family or people. Every person in the world may become a Muslim if he so chooses, by his personal decision alone. His initiation into Islam needs no partaking of any sacrament, no participation by any clergy and no

---

* (ṢAAS) – *Ṣallā Allāhu ʿalayhi wa sallam*: May the peace and blessings of God be upon him. Said whenever the name of the Prophet Muhammad is mentioned.

confirmation by any organized body. As to "Islamicity," therefore, all men are absolutely equal in that the house of Islam may be entered by all and everyone upon his satisfying the simplest of requirements. In the matter of men being Muslims or non-Muslims, there is no middle ground, no ambiguity, no complication.

Great as it may be in the eye of Islam for any person to make the decision to enter the faith, his entry constitutes no guarantee of personal justification in the eye of God. Since Islam has no sacraments, there is nothing the new initiate can do which, if his life were to terminate at its very moment, he would be assured of salvation. Augustine's terrible case of the two newborn babies, the one going to Paradise because he received baptism and the other condemned to eternal fire because he did not, is not a problem for Islam. In Islam, justification in the eye of God is a function of man's deeds or works, not of any sacrament of which he may have partaken. Is justification, on the other hand, a function of man's personal faith? No, answers Islam. Faith is presupposed in the man's entry into the community of Islam. But faith may be a mere statistical feature, a mark of social self-identification. It may and may not produce the works of virtue, the deeds of righteousness. Only the latter, therefore, constitutes justification.

On the scale of virtue and righteousness, men occupy varying positions. The scale itself is infinite; and there is no point at which a Muslim may carry his title to Paradise, as it were, in his pocket. Everyone strives and some strive more than others. Judgment by God of any man's fate is not pre-empted by anything any individual can do, whether for or against salvation. For God may reject the greatest deeds because of lack of faith and seriousness on the part of their doer; and He may forgive the greatest sinner. Likewise, He is not determined to pass favorable judgment on anyone by virtue of his partaking in any "sacrament." The Muslim is hence a person who, having joined the ranks of Islam by his solemn witnessing, is engaged in the pursuit of righteousness the rest of his life. The simple test of Islamicity provided by Islamic law, designed to make entry into Islam the easiest religious passage ever devised, is balanced by a salvation requisite, after entry, which is by nature infinite and hence never fully satisfied. Religious justification is thus the Muslim's eternal hope, never his complacency, not even for a fleeting moment. The Muslim, therefore, is a person who, as his solemn witnessing has indicated, believes that only God is God and Muhammad is His Prophet. That only God is God makes of him at once the humblest and proudest creature. He is humble, and rubs his proud forehead against the ground in prostration, before God. God is to him, the One Creator, Provider, Ruler, Forgiver and Judge, the First Cause and the Final End of everything, the Ultimate Reality. He is the object of adoration and praise, of thanks and worship, the One Master to Whom all one's life is devoted in dedication and service. The Muslim is the proudest of people precisely because of this loyalty to God. Besides God, no thing and no man is worthy of his loyalty, of his service and work. The Muslim may not submit to any ruler, and much less to any tyrant, because his submission is all due to the One Master. Some Muslims indeed do submit to rulers and tyrants; but they do so at the cost of violating their very definition as Muslims. In this submission to God, the Muslim places himself on a par with the whole of mankind, which he regards as equally obliged to recognize the Creator of all. He is touched by a feeling of strongest brotherhood to any person so submitting himself to the divine Sovereign; for *vis-à-vis* the Creator, there is no perspective or category, no bond or definition, mightier and more proper than that of creatureliness. Here all human beings stand absolutely identical.

Equally, and on account of his acknowledgment of God alone as Master, the Muslim is a sort of revolutionary who champions the cause of human freedom against human masters everywhere. Nothing is more hateful to him than *shirk* or associating other beings with God. When a person sets up money, sex, power, or pleasure as his God besides God, it is indeed bad. But when a Caesar or a tyrant so sets himself up and demands absolute loyalty from the citizens – loyalty belonging exclusively to God – then rebellion against that ruler and his ultimate overthrow become for the Muslim a prime religious objective.

The Muslim believes that God has created man and the world not in sport, and certainly not in vain, but for a purpose. This purpose is that man may fulfill his ethical vocation; that he may do the good deeds. The scripture of Islam pictures the life of man *in* the world as a free competition among men for doing the better, the nobler, the greater deeds. On this account, it called man "*khalīfah*" or vicegerent of God, i.e., he who acts and fulfills, on behalf of God. The world God created is one which fits this moral vocation of man, one in which man is efficacious, where the realization of goodness, truth and beauty is actually possible.

This purpose is what gives meaning to the Muslim's life. And there can be no greater meaning than to serve as the actualizer of God's will on earth, as the realizer of goodness and value in space and time. It is the source of his dignity and self-esteem. In fact, it does assign him a cosmic status to see himself, on a par with all other men, as the bridge through which the moral good must pass to be actualized on earth. Realization of the moral good requires that it be achieved in freedom, i.e., under conditions where it is equally possible for man to realize as well as to violate the moral imperative. Only the human being, of all creatures on earth, is so equipped.

To be a *khalīfah*, or vicegerent of God on earth, is no little burden. First, the task the position imposes is world-wide. Everything in creation is object of improvement. This means that the task involves the turning of every corner of the earth into all that it ought to be, namely, into a Paradise. Equally, it means that upon the Muslim falls the task of educating and transforming mankind, not only himself, his children, next of kin or compatriots, and to arrange for them the fulfillment by each of all his personal potential. All the problems of mankind are hence the Muslim's problems. To accept them, to seek morally-worthy solutions of them and to work out these solutions in history, is the Muslim's obligation and destiny – as well as his pride. Islam wants man to confront these problems head-on, and assures him that God will grant merit, and hence reward and felicity, in direct proportion to man's commitment to the task, to his engagement in the job, to his success in achieving the divine purpose of creation – namely, the universal and highest good of all men, of all peoples, of all things. All of the Muslim's life is to be lived in service to God; that is, in educating and disciplining himself, in discovering the laws of nature so as to make his usufruct of it possible and easy; and finally, in living and enabling every person and thing to live the divine pattern which is God's will. The

What is a Muslim?

Muslim is he who interferes with every natural process so as to make it serve man's needs and fulfill his joys; who interferes with the life of everyone on earth so as to enable that person better to fulfill his potential, to realize to the full his noble destiny as God's vicegerent. Obviously, to live the life of Islam is to live dangerously. But it is also to live with the highest expectation, the greatest promise, the deepest joy of which man is capable.

CHAPTER 3

Why is the Muslim
a Muslim?

THAT God is sole Creator and Master of the world, that He is the First Cause and Final End, that man is His servant, that human service is the kneading and molding of the world and of man into what it and he ought to be, and that such work is possible and upon its completion depends man's felicity and bliss – all this is Islam's view of reality. This view is not without grounds and justification; nor is it devoid of problems.

The first striking characteristic of Islam is that its view is wholly positive. It seems to prescribe the doing of the good, and trusts that the moral imperatives can and would be obeyed. But isn't man by nature inclined to do the opposite, to do evil? Isn't his nature to sin, defy God and disobey the moral commandments? Isn't he a "fallen" creature in need of ransom and salvation before he can be expected to do the good?

That man is by nature inclined to sin, defy God and disobey Him is certainly true, answers Islam. But it is equally true that man's nature is also to obey God, to do the good and act ethically. The two are possible for him, and he inclines to the one as much as he does to the other. The fact that he can do evil when he does the good, and can do the good when he does evil, adds a new dimension to his worth or unworth when he does either. If he were compelled, i.e., without freedom, to follow a single course, his action would be neither moral nor immoral, though it might have realized a material value or disvalue. No man is hopelessly bound to one or the other course of action; and if he were, no one in his senses would consider him morally responsible.

Man, therefore, is no more "fallen" than he is "saved." Because he is not "fallen," he stands in no need for a savior; and because he is not "saved," he stands in need to do the good works and do them ethically, which alone would earn him the desired "salvation." Indeed, "salvation" is an improper term, since one must be in a necessary predicament beyond the hope of ever pulling himself out of it, to need "salvation." That is precisely what man does not need. Man is not impotent ethically; nor is he a helpless puppet capable of neither good nor evil. He is capable of both. To "save" himself by his deeds and works is his pride and glory. To miss his chance and pass all the opportunities by, is pitiable neglect; to miss the calling deliberately and to do evil is to earn punishment, to deserve damnation.

Islam teaches that man is born innocent, and remains so until he makes himself guilty by his own deed. It does not believe in "original sin;" and its scripture interprets Adam's disobedience as his own personal misdeed; a misdeed for which he repented and which God had forgiven.

Rather than demoralize man by declaring him born with necessary, inescapable sin, Islam reassures him, that God Who does not work in vain has created him fitted for the job of vicegerent. He has given him his eyes and ears, his senses of touch and taste and smell, his discerning heart and mind, his imagination and memory, all to the end of discovering and understanding the divine pattern in creation. He has built him as He did, with grasping fingers, hurrying feet, springing muscles and supporting bones, to the end that he may manufacture, grasp or produce what he needs. He placed him on an earth receptive to his efficacy, where he can get things done. Finally, He gave him mastery over the whole of creation, for He made everything subservient to man. Even the sun, the moon and the millions of far away stars were created expressly for his benefit. Instead of being damned before he walks on earth, Islam teaches that man is blessed with all these "perfections," with life and mastery over all things, and is hence all the more expected to fulfill the divine will in his life.

Islam denies therefore that God had to ransom man by means of oblation and sacrifice. Such view, it holds, does violence to both God and man, compromising the transcendence of the former and the moral status of the latter. It regards Jesus as God's prophet, sent to teach identically the same message as all other prophets and to reform the Jews who had gone astray from the same teaching delivered to them by those prophets. It holds the Christians, not Jesus, accountable for what is being taught in his name. But it reassures them that they are essentially in the right, especially when they call men to worship God and to serve Him by doing the good works. Moreover, Islam explains their "mistake" as due to the loss of the authentic texts of revelation. Profiting from their experience, Islam preserved the absolute integrity and authenticity of its own revealed text, explaining that God Himself has sent it down, and He alone is its guardian and keeper.

If all prophets have conveyed one and the same message, whence come all the religions of history? Islam answers, there can be no difference in the message since their source is one, namely God, and since in their creatureliness, that is *vis-à-vis* God, all men are alike. Revelation through the prophets constitutes a fiduciary fund of truth for every people, since God had made His will known to every people in their own language. Variations of space and time, acculturation by alien influences and the whims and passions of men did the rest. The result was the religions of history, none of which has preserved the original text of its revelation. In their pristine purity, the revelations were one and the same and contained the same principles of religion and ethics. If they differed at all, they did so in the concrete prescriptions they imposed as implementive of those essential principles. They were one in their "what," but many in their "how." The former is their core and essence and is universal and eternal; the latter is accidental and is relative to the circumstances of history, to the peculiarities of the specific people to whom it was sent.

Paralleling the eternal "what" is a built-in capacity in every human being to recognize God and grasp His will as the good and ought of morality. This is not merely man's endowment with the senses and reason we have mentioned earlier. Besides all these, there is a sixth sense, which all men share in common, a genuine *sensus communis*, which enables them all to perceive God. Awareness of the holy is innate to man. There is no man without religion, and no religion without the holy. If men saw the holy in different forms, that is due to their upbringing, their legacies of culture and religion. In its pure form, the *sensus numinis* in every man makes him aware of God, the Holy One, and of His will as the moral imperative. It is hence for more than one reason that God holds all men equally responsible before Him.

Conversely, man ought to regard and treat all other men as his equals. In acting morally, i.e., in fulfilling the divine will, man should aim at the whole of humanity. Certainly considerations of nearness and strategy impose upon him to start his good "works" at home, beginning with himself. But granted these necessities, he cannot discriminate between the human creatures of God. Whether as subjects of moral action, or as objects of moral action by others, all men are equal because they are all equally creaturely, their creatureliness being the ground of their obligation to serve God. Universalism is God-given as well as God-enjoined.

Within the Semitic family of nations in which Islam was born, the Jews have admirably preserved the revealed teaching that God is transcendent and One. However, Islam charged them with misunderstanding divine transcendence when they thought of God as related to themselves in a way other than He is related to all other creatures. Their teaching of a doctrine of divine election which put them ahead of all men in receiving God's favors, Islam found objectionable. They held themselves to be God's children and elect regardless of their deeds. In so doing they were the object of Islam's castigation and chastisement. Islam regarded itself as the religion of Abraham, Jacob, Moses and David as each of them conveyed the revealed message in its pure and unadulterated form. In consequence, the Muslim identified himself with the Jews as worshipper and servant of one and the same transcendent God and regarded his own religious doctrine as Judaism purged of all ethno-centrism and especially, of the doctrines of election and of the "remnant." As far as Jewish law and ethics are concerned, Islam confirmed the revelation of Jesus insofar as it removed the yoke of literalism and legalism which the Jewish tradition had spun around the Law of Moses, and revoked the laws which the rabbis had added to it.

Religious authority, Islam held, belongs only to God. As tyrants are condemned and men are enjoined to shake off their tyranny, the road to God should be an open and free highway, admission to which has only one requisite, namely creatureliness. Away, therefore, Islam taught, with priesthood and all its orders and men. The tasks of teaching the truth, of guiding the young and counseling the erring, will last as long as man. But they constitute universal duties equally incumbent on all men. Prestige in the discharge of these tasks belongs to whomsoever has acquired the most and highest learning which is itself accessible to all. The ages-long occupation of priests as intermediaries between God and man has in Islam come to an end. God is the Forgiver, Punisher, Judge and Master, not the priest. He does not delegate these functions to any creature because that would violate His transcendence and role as sole governor and judge of men. He is close, near, fully responsive to every man's prayer. His mercy and care for mankind, along with His omnipotence, demand that all men address themselves directly to Him. God needs no bureaucracy.

Priesthood fulfills the function of administering the sacraments. Sacrament, however, is precisely what Islam, like Judaism before it, denies and condemns. A sacrament is a celebration through which man's prayer is addressed to God, and an aspect of God's power which is channeled back to man, through the mediation of a priest. Islam holds both avenues to be false: man's prayer reaches to God without need for intermediaries; and no aspect whatever of God's power or divinity is channeled anywhere without threat to divine transcendence. God's power and sanctity are solely God's. They are not dispensed to any creature because Creator and creature are two absolutely disparate kinds of being which never fuse into each other. Perhaps one can say that life as a whole is one sacrament insofar as God is the source of life, and man's life is a song of praise to God, a discharge of His commandment, a sort of "return" to Him. But even that is the end of sacrament in the meaning of fragmentation and diffusion of divinity. Doing away with the priesthood obviates the sacrament of ordination, and doing away with the sacraments obviates the need for priests. Without original sin, there is no need for baptism; and with God being in direct control of human affairs, worshippers, thanks-givers, confessors and supplicators can all address themselves directly to the divine Presence.

It is God who indeed is the Master, the sole Master. He alone is the Judge, and He knows all since nothing escapes His Mastery. It is not in any man's hand to dispense His power. Judgment of a man's whole life, or of any of his deeds, is God's prerogative, not man's. And it is the consummating conclusion of human life when, on the Day of Judgment, every man is meted out the exact reward or punishment he has earned in his life. In the view of Islam, the "other world" or the "other kingdom" has no other meaning than this consummation. It is not another world, another space-time, designed to supplant this world, this space-time, and to make up for us all the deficiencies and shortcomings of this world. Inheriting the view from Zoroastrianism, Judaism maintained that in the other world, the absolute good would be realized which was lost forever in this world, and which would never be realized in this world. Such is based upon the view that the Kingdom of David was itself the Kingdom of God, and that God would send a messiah to restore it cataclysmically at the end of time. Following in the same path, Christianity went one step further by indi-cating this world and all time as hopelessly fallen and depraved, and hence utterly impossible to be a realm where the absolute good might be realized. It projected the other world as an idealized substitute, where nothing but sweetness, joy and bliss would befall the "saved." Islam rejected both views as demoralizing to man's faith in himself, in this world. Reasserting the essential innocence and goodness of both man and the world, Islam taught not only that the realization of the absolute is possible in this world but that to bring it about here and now is precisely the duty of every man and woman. It warned mankind that there is no world other than this; that there is no space-time other than this; that all man's duties and hopes are to be fulfilled in this world – if they are to be fulfilled at all.

This world, the Muslim believes, is the realm of God, the Kingdom wherein utopia is possible of actualization if man performs his duty and responds to the divine call with obedience. God wishes for man to do the good deeds, and the good deeds do actually transform this world into the ideal; that this was from the beginning the whole purpose of creation, rather than the fall or defeat of that original purpose. The other world, Islam holds, is not "another" world, an alternative to this world, but merely a consummation of judgment passed on whether or not we willed to transform this world and succeeded in so doing. It would be totally different from, and hence "other" than, this world, not because our present frustrations and deprivations will be satisfied, but because it will be transcendent, i.e., beyond this space and this time. It is not, however, a "world;" it has no dimension; and it is not a replica of this world with its sorrows turned into joys. It is Paradise or Hell in the sense of reward or punishment, a consummation of reward and punishment meted out in judgment.

Only such a view, Islam holds, is consistent with loyalty to this world. Without it, this world would become merely a bridge or passage on which we are transients, advised neither to tarry nor to build but quickly to get to the other shore. This is denial of this world. Islam, on the other hand, is world-affirming, stressing this as the only world. We either succeed or fail in it, doing the right or the wrong. Being free and responsible, everything we do in this world counts for us or against us. On the Day of Judgment, which will also be the termination of this world, we would be given what we have deserved, blessedness or damnation. Piety and morality, that is, obedience to God, should be our choice in this world for a double reason: they do bring us happiness and acknowledge utopia in this world; they also and at the same time promise us blessedness on the Day of Judgment, for they are indeed obedience to God. That is why Islam, Muslims hold, achieves for man two happinesses: happiness here and happiness in the hereafter. (Qur'an 2:201)

CHAPTER 4

Since When is Anyone a Muslim?

ISLAM began as a world religious movement in the first decade of the seventh century of the Common Era, in the city of Makkah in Arabia. It was taught by Muhammad, son of ʿAbdullāh, of the tribe of Quraysh, who at the ripe age of forty, began to have visions in which God, through the instrumentality of Angel Gabriel, sent down a revelation. The revelation was from God, not of God. It was a disclosure of His will, or commandments, in sublime Arabic form. It came piecemeal, sometimes in a problematic situation which called for a solution, dispensation or guidance for the given circumstance, sometimes without, the situation being the wider religious context of the unbelievers, or of the Christians and Jews of whom there were many in Arabia and the adjoining countries. At first, Muhammad himself did not believe, and thought the matter to be an illusion, a devil's temptation or possession. As the visions persisted, he became convinced that God was truly calling him to rise and teach the new faith.

The first convert was Muhammad's wife, whose faithfulness to her husband made her a Muslim before Muhammad's conviction of his own prophethood. Other relatives and friends followed and a nucleus community was formed. The Arabs, whose traditional faith denied the unity and transcendence of God as well as the Day of Judgment and who based life on some chivalry values, hedonism and materialism were not responsive. At first, they subjected the new teaching to scorn; but when Muhammad and his companions stood firm, they countered with subversion, public vituperation and persecution. The fledging community bore its travail with patience and determination and continued to grow. Soon, the Arab hierarchy in Makkah decided that there was no escape from total war against the new Muslims if their and Makkah's position in the religious, social, political and economic spheres were to be saved. They offered Muhammad wealth, kingship of Makkah and cure of his "madness" by the greatest physicians of the world. But he refused. Then they sought to break up the tribal solidarity of Muhammad's clan of Hāshim on which the Muslims depended for inter-tribal security, by appealing to the Prophet's uncle and personal protector, the non-Muslim Abū Ṭālib, Hāshim's elder statesman, to relinquish his tribal solidarity with Muhammad. The old uncle pleaded with his nephew to cease to raise trouble which the clan could no longer bear. But the Prophet answered: "If the sun was put in my right hand and the moon in the left in exchange for God's religion, I would never yield − not even if I were to perish in preaching it!" When that too failed, the Makkans put in operation a plot to assassinate Muhammad.

Sensing danger, Muhammad had contracted with Muslim converts from Madinah to furnish protection in case of need. When danger came close, he outwitted his enemies and slipped out of Makkah to join the Muslim followers of Madinah, now reinforced with the Muslims of Makkah who had emigrated to Madinah, one after the other, at the advice of the Prophet. In Madinah, the danger did not disappear, but took a more ominous turn. Now it became a real war between Makkah and Madinah and all the tribes of the countryside which the two powers could rally to their sides.

Upon arrival in Madinah, Muhammad integrated the Muslims of all tribes into one solid body, and integrated this body with the Jews of Madinah into an Islamic polity. He gave it its constitution and assumed its leadership. The revelations continued to come providing guidance in the social, political, economic and judicial affairs with which Muhammad had to deal. The war with Makkah began with skirmishes, which were followed by two main rounds of battle, one of which was gained by each party, but neither of which was conclusive enough to enable the victor to put a final end to the hostility. A truce followed, before and during which Islam won the adherence of thousands. When allies of Makkah violated the truce, the Muslims mobilized and marched on Makkah, conquering it without a fight. In a magnanimous gesture, Muhammad forgave the Makkans; and they converted to Islam *en masse*. The Prophet entered the Ka'bah, the House which Abraham and his son Ismail built for worship of the One God and which had by then become filled with idols. He destroyed the idols and images, cleansed and reconsecrated the House to God.

One campaign after another was now launched to bring Islam to the remaining tribes of Arabia. Some felt now free from the might of pagan Makkah, and free to give conscientious consideration to the call of Islam. These joined the ranks of Islam voluntarily. Others felt strong enough to continue the fight without Makkah, and had to be brought into line by force. Converts to Islam, however, did not come only from pagan Arabian religion. Arab Christians and Jews converted in significant numbers. Those who rejected Islam and stood firm by their old faith, whether Judaism or Christianity, were not molested. On the contrary, under divine sanction revealed in the Qur'an, the Prophet had recognized Christianity, Judaism and the religion of the Sabaeans as revealed and valid, fraternized with their followers, and integrated them within the Islamic state even while they preserved their religion, their culture, their customs and their non-Muslim identities. The Islamic State was their protector. They lived under its aegis as religiously, culturally and legally autonomous units, complete communities with their own schools, temples, law courts and leaderships. The whole of Arabia, however, stood at the death of the Prophet in 632 CE – ten years after the hijrah (emigration) of the Prophet to Madinah – united and poised to carry the message of Islam to the world. Muhammad had previously sent messengers to the leaders of the then-known world inviting them to join Islam; or, if they wished, to keep their religion but join the new world-order of Islam which was built on the principle of free movement of man, ideas and wealth anywhere. Some answered with friendship and sympathy; others, by beheading the messengers.

The next one hundred years saw the most spectacular conquests history has ever witnessed. The Muslims stood in France and Spain after a sweep across North Africa; in Central Asia and the Indus River basin in the East, after a lightning sweep across the Persian Empire. The two greatest empires of the time, Persia and Byzantium had crumbled and failed. More spectacular yet was the tremendous appeal of the new world view of Islam to Christians torn apart for centuries by Byzantine theological controversies, and Persians broken with suffering under the yoke of caste and a very unjust socio-religious system. Within a generation men and women converted to Islam by the millions.

The great appeal of Islam consisted in the reasonableness of its theological claim. The world was created by God, the One and only Transcendent Being, Who implanted therein His pattern, thus making it an orderly cosmos. He also created man rational, free and responsible, that by exercising his faculties, he may achieve the good in this world, in all the world, and for all men in equality and brotherhood. That all men are equal means that there shall be no heretication, no coercion in religion, as well as no imperialist colonization of one people by another. God does not want man to mortify himself, nor to lead the ascetic or monastic life. Rather he should lead an abundant life, full of joy and happiness, but realizing the moral laws of purity, faithfulness to God, equity and fairness, love and brotherhood. Man is destined to serve God in His earth, to build it up and fructify it; for it is good and capable of actualizing man's idealistic vision. To do so and persevere is to guarantee success and happiness in this world as well as on the Day of Judgment. There is neither vicarious sin, nor vicarious guilt, nor vicarious suffering, nor vicarious punishment, nor vicarious merit and salvation. Blest or unblest, every soul gets exactly what it has deserved, according to its personal deeds.

Moreover, what left the worldwide audience of the Islamic call utterly armless and won their hearts to Islam without resistance was the fact that the Muslims really practiced what they taught. There was no splitting of personality, no double conscience, no hypocrisy, no racialist inequality however camouflaged. The Muslim readily intermarried with the citizens of other lands even before their conversion to Islam, a measure which raised the vanquished to the status of in-laws of the conqueror. Muslim rationalism and pragmatism knew few bounds, as Muslims pursued knowledge and wisdom at the feet of non-Muslim masters without shame or self-conceit. They paid double attention to prove their faith true, that is, that Islam indeed gives its adherents two happinesses, here and in the hereafter. (Qur'an 2:201)

This avid pursuit of the two happinesses resulted in worldly wisdom and success for the Muslims as well as moral felicity. It caused Muslim science, engineering, arts and letters to prosper and flourish; their empire to succeed; and their moral record to remain, on the whole impeccable. This instilled in the hearts of non-Muslims a deep sense of respect and admiration for Islam's followers, and a yearning to emulate or join them. When a decision to join was voiced by any non-Muslim, of however lowly an origin or status, to enter Islam, he was instantly raised to the highest level, declared a brother to all the believers, intermarried with them, and received with open arms in genuine brotherhood. For these reasons, the state income from the *jizyah*, the poll tax all able, lay, adult, male non-Muslims paid to the Islamic state in lieu of the zakah tax and military service imposed on all Muslims, dwindled in the first fifty years after the conquests from numerous millions of dinars to a trifle – because of these massive conversions to Islam!

The spring and summer of the Islamic Empire lasted five hundred years, during which the Muslims led the world in everything – astronomy to spices. They discovered new lands and established new disciplines. In the meantime, their energies were spent, and they began to decline on many fronts. Internal division weakened them before their foes; individualism, and preoccupation with personal salvation weakened the internal cohesion of state and society. Finally, misunderstanding of spiritual welfare as the gnosis of the mystics dulled the Muslim's rational powers, removed him from empirical and pragmatic enquiry, and delivered him to the esoteric whimsy of the *shaykh, pir* or mystic elder.

At the same time, the greatest holocaust of history was unleashed by the Mongols of Central Asia against the world. Unfortunately, the Islamic Empire was the first obstacle standing in the way of the rampaging hordes. They fell on it with fire and fury, razing city after city and ravaging province after province. At the same time, European crusaders fell on the Empire from the West. While the Empire managed finally to repulse the crusaders, islamize the Mongols and acculturate all invaders who chose not to return whence they came, the majority of Muslims became conservative out of fear for the extinction of their faith, and withdrawn from history out of preoccupation with "eternity." As the reconquest of Spain by Europe became imminent from the beginning of the fourteenth century, islamized elements of the eastern invaders, still stirring with energy and power, took to the field to rebuild the stricken empire. Within a generation, the empire was on its feet, marching again in the direction of Europe as Europe was marching through Spain. The Muslims conquered Asia Minor and Constantinople fell in 1458 CE Europe stopped in Spain; but the Muslims pushed forward until, a century later, they laid siege to Vienna, having appropriated all the territories in between as well as the whole of the Caucasus, southern Russia and Poland.

The mystic disease was kept at bay during two or three centuries, but it was not uprooted. The new empire fell easy prey to it, and the same drama of internal and external weakness was repeated. Europe not only recovered, but grew strong enough to repulse the Muslims from its territories (except for the Muslim communities of Albania, Yugoslavia and other Balkan countries). Europe's forces occupied the whole Muslim World except Central Arabia and Yemen, and divided it among themselves. The Muslim World groaned under colonial rule for a century at places, and for three centuries at others.

The wind of reform and reconstruction stirred within the heart of Arabia, as it did in earlier centuries. Out of the desert came calls to repudiate mysticism and return to the life-and-civilization-giving views of pristine Islam. The Muslim World responded with a whole series of movements designed to cleanse and raise Islamic society. These movements soon became political, as colonialist Europe mobilized to stop them. Quickly, the battle lines were drawn: On one side stood Europe, fighting to spread the religion of Christ with the imperial sword, and to protect its exploitation of Muslim lands and labor as well as the colonialist settlers which had been planted among the Muslims. On the other side stood the Muslim World, defending the traditional native faith of the fathers against foreign aggression, protecting the land and people against alien invasion, occupation and colonial settlement.

Today the competition has barely shifted from military confrontation to economic, neo-colonial, and other more subtle means of subversion and exploitation. The Muslim World is modernizing and industrializing at a furious pace, leaping over centuries. The Western Christian World is overdeveloped and needs both the material and human resources of the other. What was a handful of Muslims in the Christian West fifty years ago, is now a considerable stream of immigrants taking up positions in factories as well as in universities. Today there is an Islamic presence in Europe and America that has become native and is certain to grow.

The next door neighbor in any metropolitan center in Europe and North America might well be a Muslim. He may be caucasian or colored; he may speak any one of a dozen Islamic languages besides English. And he may be so Westernized and acculturated that one may not easily become aware of his presence without communicating with him.

Part II

Moments of the
Muslim's Religious Life

CHAPTER 5

Shahādah
(The Confession of Faith)

THE Muslim confesses that there is no god but God and that Muhammad is the Prophet of God. This confession is called *shahādah* or "witness." It is not only his legal passport into the Muslim community; it is the quintessence of his faith and expression of his identity, which he recites many times a day on many different occasions. Besides the principles its first half implies (justification by works, humility and submission to God, defiance of tyrants and other gods, vicegerency of man on earth, and self-fulfillment, which we discussed in chapter 2), the *shahādah* asserts the prophethood of Muhammad. This means that the witness accepts what Muhammad has conveyed from heaven as truly what God has sent down. These revelations collected together in the order the Prophet himself has directed them to be recited, constitute the Holy Qur'an, the scripture of Islam. To witness that Muhammad is the Prophet of God is tantamount to witnessing that the Qur'an is the holy word of God, complete, *verbatim* and in the order it has been collected; that its commandments and directives are normative, incumbent on the Muslim as God's ever-present pronouncement.

The Prophet enjoys a second kind of authority, beside that of conveying the holy word of God *verbatim*. That is the authority of actualizing the revelation in his own life. His life, with its deeds and decisions, approbations and condemnations, constitutes the perfect embodiment of the Islamic message. The Prophet's Sunnah ("trodden path," or "example") is therefore normative to the Muslim and constitutes the exemplary "how" for the "what" of revelation. From it, the Muslim derives all his liturgy as well as a fair measure of the precepts of Islamic law and ethics. The Sunnah has come down to us as reports carried by the Prophet's companions and passed to the generations after them. These reports are called hadith(s).

The authenticity and integrity of the text of the Qur'an stand beyond question. The Qur'anic revelations came in the full light of history, were both written down and memorized by the thousands among a people with the most developed memory in the world. Ever since they were revealed, they were continuously recited in public, in front of people who were perfectly familiar with them throughout the Muslim World. Believing that he is reciting the *ipissima verba* of God, the Muslim gave his recitation and his copying of the Qur'anic text absolutely the greatest care. Even the very act of worship, the formal prayer, which may not be interrupted for any reason – not even by a threat to the worshipper's security – because in prayer the Muslim is supposed to stand in the presence of God, may be interrupted and the worship leader corrected aloud by anyone listening, whenever a fault occurs in the recitation of the Holy Qur'an. Finally, at the very time the Caliph ʿUthmān (644-656 CE) was collecting and promulgating the present text of the Qur'an as a book, internal strife and contest for power split the community asunder. For decades and centuries since, the factions continued their bloody strife, each justifying its case with arguments and quotations from the Holy Book. Never has anyone claimed or accused the other of tampering with the text. This was a final test of fire which the Qur'anic text has passed with flying colors. That is why Sir William Muir reported von Hammer's scholarly judgment approvingly that, "we [scholars] are as certain that the Qur'an is the historical word of Muhammad as the Muslim is certain it is the word of God."

The texts of the Sunnah do not enjoy such unquestionable authority. Muslims are perfectly aware that the Sunnah has been tampered with as it was transmitted between the first four generations. Hence, they are careful always to qualify the Sunnah with the word *al-ṣaḥīḥah* (i.e., "veritable" or "verified"). To sift the veritable from the weak or spurious hadiths, Muslims have perfected the sciences of textual criticism and elaborated the most sophisticated disciplines to criticize and ascertain the historical veritability of the chains of narrators, of every hadith, of the form or language, of the redaction of the text, of the coherence and rationality of the content of the text and its correspondence with the Holy Qur'an, with otherwise known historical reality and the accumulated wisdom of mankind. Their love and respect for the hadiths of the Prophet knew no bounds. Hence, they preserved all the materials claimed to come from the Prophet, but they classified them into a long series of categories of ascending or descending levels of authenticity.

The Prophethood of Muhammad, restricting itself to the *verbatim* conveyance of the word of God, presents us with a perfection of the whole phenomenon of prophecy in Semitic culture. Certainly Moses represented another apex in that history, after which prophecy degenerated in Israel to the point of there being hundreds of pseudo-prophets running in the market places without any being able to prove his prophethood conclusively. Islam restituted prophecy to its place of high honor. The change in times however prescribed that prophets no longer justify themselves with miracles which boggle the mind, or reason, of man. Hence, Islam believes in no miracles and Muslims claim none for Muhammad. In their view, what proves Muhammad's prophethood is the sublime beauty and greatness of the revelation itself, the Holy Qur'an, not any inexplicable breaches of natural law which confound man's reason or pass his powers of understanding. The Qur'anic revelation is a presentation to man's mind, to reason. It makes its claim critically. It is not a "scandalon" or "stumbling block." Instead of commanding blind belief, it invites man to consider the evidence, to compare and contrast the claims and the data, and to judge only in certainty and conviction of the truth.

This is why Islam never had a religious synod or council or church empowered with the right of *magisterium*, the right to make *ex cathedra* pronouncements about Islam. In Islam, religious truth is a matter of argument and conviction, a cause in which everybody is entitled to contend and everybody is entitled to convince and be convinced. To witness that Muhammad is the Prophet of God means in final analysis that one is convinced of the truth and viability of the claim that religious truth is critical, arguable and self-convincing. This categorically affects the first part of the *shahādah*, namely, "There is no god but God." It tells us that this is a rational claim; and we can convince ourselves of its truth neither by authority nor coercion. We have to reason, to think and consider all the evidence, in seriousness and responsibility. Even if we were tentatively to deny it, we can do so only under the proviso that truth is possible to know, that it is, like God, one and not many. But isn't God the truth?

CHAPTER 6

Salah
(Worship, Prayer)

THE word salah is better translated as "worship" than "prayer." Prayer, it is well known, is not necessarily formal. It has no prescribed style, and can be recited almost anywhere, anytime. It is not obligatory, like the sacrament of communion in Christianity, or indispensable like baptism. Islam knows a form of communion with God which fits the appellation "prayer," and it is called *du'ā'*, literally invocation or calling. Like "prayer," it varies according to the content, as in prayer of thanksgiving, of praise, of supplication, of forgiveness, etc.

Unlike *du'ā'*, salah has a definite and precise form. It has to be recited five times a day at given intervals. If the time assigned to it is missed, it can be made up, but under the express consciousness that one is only making up what has been missed. It is an absolute commandment of God imposed upon all adult Muslims, male and female. There is no Islam without it, if it is denied defiantly. If it is neglected, the Muslim has committed a grave sin which must be repented and made up. However, no Muslim has authority to force an adult to hold it; and no one may prosecute or charge with heresy, a Muslim for delinquency in its performance unless that delinquency is accompanied by public defiance of the commandment enjoining it.

Salah is preceded by ablution. This is both real and symbolic, and both levels of meaning are required in Islam. The Muslim may not approach the divine Presence, as he does in salah, with a dirty body or appearance. Just as the place where he prays is required to be clean (and hence the ubiquitous "prayer" rug throughout the world of Islam), so his clothing and body must be equally clean. Soiled clothes have to be changed. Hands, mouth and teeth, nose, face, head, neck and ears, arms to the elbows and feet to the ankle, have to be washed in clean, preferably running, water. The whole operation must be preceded with a silent declaration of intention to oneself that one is entering into it for the sake of God.

As far as physical cleanliness is concerned, ablution is a welcome exercise. We can appreciate its prophylactic value when applied to desert people where dust abounds, and to farmers in irrigated lands where mud is the order of the day, everyday. But we can also appreciate its blessings in our industrial cities where soot and other air polluting agents threaten to choke us. Psychologists everywhere would applaud its refreshing and rejuvenative effect as it comes at dawn, noon, mid-afternoon, sunset and night. As to its symbolic meaning, it is a ritual whose purpose is self-preparation for communion with God. The *niyyah*, or declaration of intent, which precedes it, sets the mood for seriousness and gravity, as man approaches the precincts of the Holy.

Salah can be performed anywhere; for wherever the Muslim stands, there is God present. No ground is holy; and the mosque is only a place dedicated for worship, but not "consecrated." Salah can be performed by the worshipper alone, since there is no sacrament and no priesthood in Islam. Performing it with one's fellows is desirable, not obligatory; but obligatory is the Muslim's performance of congregational salah on Friday (*jum'ah*). The congregational salah is led by an imam (leader) whose function is to synchronize the movements of beginning and ending, of genuflection and prostration. Any Muslim may lead the salah, provided his recitation of the Qur'an is correct. On Friday, the imam delivers a *khuṭbah*, or sermon, in addition to these duties. The subject of the sermon should be a living issue in Muslim life; and the imam should try to relate the relevant passages of the Qur'an and hadith to the issue at hand.

For the congregational salah, the Qur'an advises that beautiful clothes be worn with decorum. Before starting it, the imam makes sure that the lines of worshippers are full and solid and straight. All face in the direction of the Ka'bah in Makkah. The sight of Muslims in salah, whether standing in their straight rows or kneeling and prostrating themselves, is indeed a forcefully expressive and deeply moving sight. The straight line bespeaks the equality of all, and the solid fullness, brotherhood and the community's cohesiveness.

The night ends at dawn and the day begins. Islam prescribes that the day begin with salah, where God is praised, His guidance is sought and His blessing and mercy are prayed for. Between dawn and the noon salah, there is usually a stretch of 7-8 hours which can and should be used to do the day's work. Where the work is of a heavy nature, this period is adequate to satisfy the needs of a progressive, well organized economy. Where the work is light, it can be resumed after the noon salah, which can also constitute a refreshing break. No one needs work beyond the mid-afternoon salah, unless it is for an emergency situation or for his own pleasure and desire. The sunset salah terminates the day, and the night salah marks the Muslim's retirement.

Salah is a discipline. Its ablution, its form, its movement, timing and number of genuflections and prostrations – all these constitute, exercises in self-attunement to the call of God. The Qur'an says that salah is futile unless it conduces to moral action. The fact is that salah properly performed does conduce to moral action and self-exertion in the greater cause, the cause of God. It does not only remind man of God. For its duration, five times a day, it causes man to live for a time face to face, as it were, with his Lord, Master and Creator. There can be no greater or more direct route to righteousness.

CHAPTER 7

Zakah
(Wealth Sharing)

LITERALLY, al-zakah means the sweetening. The idea it expresses is that it consists in justification, or making *ḥalāl* (legitimate, innocent, good) that which it is supposed to affect. The term can be used with a human being as object, in which case it means recommendation or acclamation. When used with wealth as its object – and that is the greater usage – it means making that wealth just, legitimate, innocent, good and worthy. Obviously, the worth zakah adds to wealth is not utilitarian, but moral.

Islam regards all wealth as belonging to God. Man may appropriate as much of it as he pleases, by all means which economic life makes possible, as long as such means do not infringe the moral law. Wealth gathering is legitimate activity as long as it implies no theft, no cheating, no coercion. Indeed, the pursuit of wealth is one of the primal concerns of man, demanded by survival (where it consists of the search for food, shelter, clothing and comfort) as well as by man's *khilāfah* or vicegerency (where its object is the planned satisfaction of one's own material needs and those of humanity.) Engagement in it fills the greatest portion of life and exhausts the greatest energies of all men, everywhere and at all times. It is the very stuff of which living consists. Its subjection to the moral law, i.e., its governance by the laws prohibiting the appropriation of any part of it without the free and deliberate consent of the other person involved in the transaction, is an absolute requirement. Without it, human life sinks to the level of the animals, of materialism and exploitation.

But even if every requirement of the moral law has been strictly observed in every step and stage of the process of wealth acquisition, the wealth achieved still needs justification on another level. This is what the institution of zakah seems to require. Granted, then, that I have violated no moral law in acquiring my wealth, *why* does Islam hold such wealth nonetheless illegitimate until I have justified it by means of zakah?

The answer is that whereas the moral law governs the acquisition of wealth, there is need for another law to govern its consumption and/or continued possession. Had there been no purpose to our life except its existence, no meaning to personal existence except the pleasure, comfort and satisfaction derivable therefrom, no demand could be made of the owner of wealth. *Laissez-faire* in wealth acquisition was the conclusion of political liberalism. *Laissez-faire* in the consumption of wealth is a necessary dictate of hedonism, utilitarianism, eudemonism and all moral theories which define the good in worldly or relative terms. Since Islam does define the good in terms of absolute laws which refer to a divine will and commandment, to a transcendent pattern which is the ultimate purpose of all moral action, it found necessary to regulate the consumption and possession of wealth.

Islam's tenet in this regard is that wealth, once acquired, ought to be shared with others in some proportion. This is equally the requirement of charity; and charity is as old as man. Is it all that Islam requires? Certainly, it is charity, answers Islam; but it is more. Charity has always been regarded as a high moral value by all mankind. Its proportion, nay its very observance, has been left to the personal discretion of the giver. True, morality has always taught that the greater the portion one shares with his fellows, the greater the merit. Jesus moved charity to higher moral grounds when he taught that the purer the motivation with which the giver gives his wealth, the greater the moral worth of the deed. With all this Islam fully agrees, recognizing this teaching of Jesus as genuine revelation from God. It called the institution *ṣadaqah*, a derivative from the act of faith itself by which man acknowledges God to be God.

No religion or morality before Islam has made charity itself obligatory in the sense of institutionalizing it and empowering somebody to levy, collect and distribute it. It is nice to have charity as a moral ideal. But what would be its worth if it remained an unobserved ideal? An ideal satisfiable by the millionaire's giving of a few pennies to the poor on the sidewalk? An ideal whose observance is subject only to one's conscience, or to God in the Hereafter, but to no regulation by man's peers in this world?

This is the need to which Islam addressed itself by the institution of zakah. You may give of your wealth to your fellow men as much as you please, when you please, in the manner you please. That is your *ṣadaqah* of which your conscience and God are the only judges. But you may not escape the requirement of giving every year 2.5 per cent of your total wealth to a corporate institution, the Islamic state, for distribution to the less fortunate, to those in need. Thus, Islam sought to preserve the moral value of charity, and to add to it the equally moral value of wealth-sharing or zakah. Its purpose was dual: to convince the wealthy that the title to his very wealth is mitigated by the title of his fellow man to life and subsistence, and to assure the needy that his fellow men will not passively see him suffer his misfortune. A bond of humanity, of fellowship, of brotherhood binds both the wealthy and the poor together. The Prophet said: "Men are like the organs of a body. When an organ suffers the whole body responds to repel the cause of suffering." The Qur'an went as far as to quote the consciousness of the need for altruistic self-exertion with religion itself. "Who is the denier of religion itself? It is he who repulses the orphan, who does not enjoin the feeding of the poor. Woe to those who observe the rituals of religion but are insensitive to the moral side of those rituals, and hence to the need of the miserable for assistance." (Qur'an 107:1-7)

CHAPTER 8

Sawm
(Fasting)

FASTING is an old religious custom. It was practiced by lay persons and clergy in ancient religions, as well as by Jews, Christians, Hindus and Buddhists. Though its purposes differed from religion to religion, there was general agreement that fasting was a self-preparation for communion with divinity.

Islam has prescribed for all healthy adult Muslims a rigorous fast: total abstention from food, drink and sex from dawn to sunset during every day of the month of Ramadan, the ninth month in the lunar year. The body may not partake of anything in any way or contact another of the opposite sex without breaking the fast. Exempted from this duty are children, persons suffering from sickness, or undergoing travel. In such cases, the exempted person was not to forego the fast but to postpone it to another, more healthy or restful time before recurrence of the following Ramadan.

Long before Islam, the month of Ramadan was regarded by the Arabs as a holy month. Its occasion imposed upon them the proscription of war and hunting, and brought about an uninterrupted peace during which travel and movement of goods across the desert were safe from attack by anyone or any tribe. The Arabs reckoned Ramadan as the month of spiritual stocktaking. Throughout its duration, they were especially keen to please, to settle old debts and disputes, to do good to their neighbors. The more morally sensitive natures among them underwent a retreat within the temple, or into their homes, in order not to disturb their concentration and meditation. Before his commission as Prophet, Muhammad was in the habit of retreating during Ramadan to Hira, a cave outside of Makkah, where he would spend several days in meditation. His wife used to send him a daily provision with a servant, knowing that her husband was devoting himself exclusively to worship.

Islam continued the tradition of dedicating the month of Ramadan to religious pursuits. Besides the fast, the Islamic tradition regarded moral and religious action during Ramadan as especially meritorious, and urged Muslims to increase their service to God during the month. It was during Ramadan that Muhammad received his first revelation.

Islam assigned to fasting two purposes; self-discipline and commiseration with the hungry of the earth. We have seen that Islam repudiates self-mortification and asceticism. In consequence, it cannot regard fasting as an ascetic self-denial valuable in and for itself or when done for the sake of God. For Islam does not believe that righteousness requires that mankind deny itself. God wishes for mankind to be free, healthy, fulfilled and happy. As philosophers might put it, going to the dentist is certainly a painful experience. One does not perform it for its own sake without assuming that suffering is the end of human life. One performs it willingly, however, if it is taken to lead to the realization of the purpose of health and well being which are the opposite of suffering. Accordingly, there is no denying that fasting is a hardship, and the question is, to what purpose did Islam impose it? It is in this purpose that the meaning of Ramadan must be sought.

Self-discipline through fasting is a religiously novel idea. Food and sex, which are the pivotal instincts of life, and whose satisfaction is a capital requirement of any social order, are precisely the most sensitive areas of human life. No threat to any other area could be more central or dangerous, more prone to alert man's consciousness in full, except the threat of death itself. Prohibition of food and sex does constitute such threat, the former to individual life and the latter to group life. Deliberate abstinence from food and sex stirs up the consciousness of imminent death to both the individual and the group, and provides ample opportunity to mobilize consciousness and launch it into combat, in defense of life.

Islam has prescribed total abstinence from food and sex from dawn to sunset precisely in order to stir up consciousness, to think of life and death, and to train the individual to resist the threat. The threat to individual and group life must be resisted; and the Muslim must be taught and trained in the art of resistance. Patience, forbearance, perseverance, steadfastness in suffering and privation, these are the qualities Islam seeks to cultivate through fasting. Conversely, the areas of food and sex are man's weakest spots as far as morality and righteousness are concerned. Almost all vice and immorality find their way into the world through these two avenues. To learn how to block them in the face of immoral use, to fortify the individual against temptation and make one's moral house impregnable through them, is equally the purpose of Islam.

For these reasons, Islam looks upon fasting as the best exercise in the art of self-mastery and discipline. To make the exercise pedagogically fruitful, Islam prescribed that the fast be broken promptly at sunset, even before the performance of the sunset salah. That is why Islam regarded every day in Ramadan as a fresh exercise or trial which, if carried successfully to sunset, may be ended with celebration, food and joy, that the abstinence and hence the exercise may be started all over again at dawn, the next day. A little indulgence at night, the Legislator seems to have thought, might even make the daytime abstinence more effective as an exercise in self-mastery than continuous denial which can quickly become habitual and hence of diluted effect. The alternation of abstinence and indulgence every day and night is far more forceful and effective.

Throughout the Muslim World, the month of Ramadan is received with joy. People uphold the fast and literally change their countenances. No time is better for articulating the social bond uniting Muslim to Muslim. At night, Muslim towns and villages are alive with togetherness and merrymaking. Lest the latter get out of hand and to keep the moral-religious lesson ever present to consciousness, Islam prescribed a special salah for the nights of Ramadan, namely, *tarāwīḥ*.

Ideally this salah, which is at least as long as all the ṣalawāt (plural of salah) of the day, would involve the recitation of the whole Qur'an in successive parts during the 29 or 30 days of the month.

The end of Ramadan is a feast called ʿId al-Fitr (feast of the breaking of the fast) which Muslims celebrate in one congregational salah in the first morning after Ramadan, and with gifts, visits with relatives and friends, food and joyful events. New clothing for young and old is imperative for salah of the ʿId al-Fitr, which is to be held in as few places as possible in order to congregate together the greatest possible number of Muslims. The joy of the feast is a culmination of moral success at the daily fast of the previous month. If the trial of the month of Ramadan has been a success in its totality, the feast is well deserved. The Muslim would have emerged "proven" in his ability to bend the pivotal forces of nature, the instincts for food and sex, to the demands of morality and religion. After a successful Ramadan, the Muslim must feel more capable and more ready to undertake any duty, any task. Like a bow, he has become more taut for the arrow.

The second purpose of fasting is commiseration with the hungry, the deprived of the earth. There is no teacher more eloquent or effective than experience. Privation is without doubt humanity's constant and greatest affliction. To undertake the fast of Ramadan is to empathize in live manner with the deprived everywhere. To enhance this lesson, Islam recommended the feeding of the neighbor, especially the poor, every day of Ramadan. It declared Ramadan the month of charity, of altruism, of neighborly love and kindness. It prescribed, as personal atonement, the feeding of sixty men for every day of Ramadan on which the fast is broken deliberately; and of two men in addition to making up the fast on other days if the fast was broken legitimately. Finally, it prescribed that no Muslim may attend the ʿId al-Fitr salah unless he has extended his charity to the poor the previous night. This is zakāt al-fiṭr (charity of fast-ending). Its amount is prescribed to be the equivalent of two meals on behalf of every member of the household. This measure helped to bring the joys of the feast to the poor and hungry as well.

This philosophy of fasting in Islam illustrates Islam's humanism and world-affirmation. Fasting, the art of self-denial par excellence, practiced by the ascetics of all religions, has here been transformed into an instrument of self-mastery, the better to conduct human life in its will and striving for the world and for life, but raised to higher levels of nobility and righteousness. The bitterness of denial, the morbidness of self-mortification, the antagonism to life, to space, to time and this world of men and women, of food and sex, are all wiped out in the Islamic experience. From his fast, the Muslim emerges refined and cleansed, the better to immerse himself in the discharge of his vicegerency in God's creation.

CHAPTER 9

Hajj
(Pilgrimage)

PILGRIMAGE is the last of the five pillars of Islam, the religious duties which constitute the fundamental duties of Islam. Whereas the first, the *shahādah* is the "entrance ticket" to Islam, salah and fasting are incumbent upon all Muslims unless they are physically incapable. Zakat is a "must" on all wealth whether it is possessed by a minor or an adult. Pilgrimage to Makkah is incumbent only upon the adult Muslim who has earned the wealth needed for the trip, has paid the zakah due on it, has fulfilled all his debts to his fellowmen, and has provided adequately for all his dependents during his projected absence.

Once the decision to undertake it is reached, pilgrimage begins with many celebrations and preparations at home. When the time comes for travel, the whole community goes out to bid the pilgrim farewell and wish him a pilgrimage acceptable to God. Upon arrival in the Hijaz and before entering Makkah al-Mukarramah (the blessed), the pilgrim sheds all his clothes and ornaments, takes a purifying ablution, and declares to God his *niyyah* or intention to perform the pilgrimage. He dons two pieces of unsewn white linen or cotton, one to cover his body from the waist down, the other from the waist up leaving the head bare. Henceforth he is not to shave or cut his hair, not to clip his finger nails, not to wear anything to distinguish him from the rest. He can, of course, change his wraps for clean ones whenever he wishes. Women wear normal dress in form of long robe, covering the body from head to foot, leaving face and hands exposed.

This clothing requirement is charged with religious meaning. The pilgrim is here to meet his Creator. He does so as a creature on par with all other human creatures of God. His wealth and social class, his political power as aristocrat, governor or king, his knowledge, wisdom and previous piety – none of these qualifications is allowed to show itself. All men are creatures, equally creaturely before God. The distinctions of history are wiped out. God is equally the Master of all, the merciful Benefactor of all, and the absolutely just Judge of all.

Pilgrims begin their ritual with a visit to *al-Ḥaram al-Sharīf*, "the noble sanctuary." They have to do so immediately upon arrival, taking no more time than what is necessary to settle down somewhere and deposit their belongings. At this first visit, they circumambulate the Kaʿbah seven times reciting a *duʿāʾ* (invocation) taught to them by the Prophet, and perform a short salah. They then proceed to Safa, whence they cover the distance to Marwah at trotting pace seven times (*al-Saʿy*), reenacting the experience of Hājar (Hagar), mother of Ismail, in her search for water after she was deposited there with her infant by Ibrāhīm, as he was bound for another migration. Hājar did eventually find water which tradition tells had sprung miraculously under Ismail's little feet. The fountain, called *Zamzam*, still gives its water to the pilgrims, many of whom take it in bottles to their distant relatives. On the second day, the pilgrims begin their journey to Arafat, a plain a few miles N.E. of Makkah where they camp. On the day of Arafat, the pilgrims stand together in prayer from the noon to the sunset salah, gathering around the very spot where Muhammad stood to deliver his farewell sermon on his last pilgrimage in the year 10 AH (632 CE).

The pilgrims then proceed to Mina where they sacrifice an animal and give its meat to the poor. They return to Makkah, stopping en route at Jamrah where they throw pebbles at a pillar symbolically representing their condemnation of the devil and his ways and reaffirming their resolution not to fall to temptation. At the sanctuary in Makkah, they repeat *al-Saʿy*, circumambulate the Kaʿbah seven times as they did at the beginning, and shed their *iḥrām*, or sacral condition by clipping their nails and hair and putting on their usual clothes. They join one another in the greatest celebration, the *Id al-Adha* (feast of the sacrifice) and prepare to visit al-Madīnah al-Munawwarah (the illuminated city of the Prophet) to pay their respects to the Prophet, buried within its mosque, who conveyed the message of God to them and led them to the life of Islam. At this time they prepare to return home. Their relatives and communities would be waiting for them with wishes of welcome and prayers that their pilgrimage has been accepted.

Failure to perform any of the rituals of pilgrimage because of sickness, accident or death, would not vitiate it; but failure to attend the standing at Arafat would. Obviously then, that ritual is the core and essence of the pilgrimage. Its meaning is simple, and is evident in the invocation which the pilgrim recites then, as well as throughout the pilgrimage. Its refrain is *Labbayka Allāhumma, Labbayka!* (At your call, O God, Here I come). God has called man to recognize God as his One Creator and Lord, to obey His commandments and serve Him. The whole ritual is nothing but the pilgrim's affirmative response to the divine call.

Since the pilgrim's affirmation of his recognition of God's Creatorship is at once his affirmation of all men's creatureliness and hence equality before God, the pilgrimage is the greatest and most eloquent embodiment of Islam's egalitarianism and universalism. Presently, every year nearly 2 million Muslims perform the pilgrimage. 1432 times since Muhammad's farewell pilgrimage, Muslims have gathered for the same rituals from the four corners of the earth. Here, in their naked human creatureliness before God, Muslims come from all races, classes, cultures, peoples, ways of life to reaffirm and renew their obedient and affirmative response to God's call. No religious event anywhere, has ever been so spectacular as Muslim pilgrimage to Makkah. None has attracted as many people; and none has expressed its religious meanings so obviously and so successfully. It was this sight that convinced Malcolm X that his black racialism was not the answer to white racialism; that a black identity asserting itself in contradistinction from Anglo-Saxon Christianity remained empty until it included the positive submission to God and to His will, to the Sharicah (Law).

Part III

Other Muslim Celebrations

CHAPTER 10

The Prophet's Birthday

THE visit which the pilgrim pays to Madinah and to the Prophet's grave is indicative of the honor and esteem in which the Prophet is held by all Muslims. The Muslim is always expected to invoke God's blessing on him whenever and wherever his name is mentioned. Such invocations are made a countless number of times a day, every day; and the salah includes it as part of the liturgy. There have been many prophets before Muhammad, and many charismatic leaders who earned the love and admiration of their people. Muhammad derived greatest love, honor and respect from the Muslims.

Certainly, some men commanded so much love and honor on the part of their adherents that the latter transformed them in their consciousness and declared them divine. The practice was common in classical antiquity as well as in India, China, Japan, and Africa. One could even venture the suggestion that there is something in human nature that tends to associate with divinity anything that is perceived as sublime. Indeed, much as Islam condemned the practice, some of the Prophet's followers fell to temptation. As the Prophet lay on his deathbed in his room, these clamored that he did not die but was lifted to heaven to join God's company. The denial of his mortality was the first but adequate step for his apotheosis. On hearing of the news of the

Prophet's death, Abū Bakr, his closest friend and constant companion, went into his room to ascertain the event and entered the mosque hall where the claim was being voiced by no less a leader than ʿUmar. After several polite but failing attempts to silence ʿUmar, Abū Bakr stood up, shoved ʿUmar aside and said to the assembled Muslims: "If any of you has been worshipping Muhammad, let him know that Muhammad is dead. But if you have been worshipping God, then know that God is eternal and never dies." This was a terribly shocking reminder to the Muslims that only God is God, only He is immortal; that Muhammad was nothing but human, all too human and mortal like everyone else. It was the last time the Muslims entertained any idea of deifying the Prophet, of lifting him above the pale of humanity.

The humanness of Muhammad is not a drawback, but an enhancement of his great merit. As a human, he received the revelation of God; and as a human he conveyed it to mankind. As a human, he understood the revelation, interpreted and exemplified it in his life. The revelation being the will of God, Muhammad's career would not be instructive had he been divine. Men would then have to struggle with the translation of divine conduct into something humanly possible, capable of human actualization. The preservation of Muhammad's humanity is the making normative of his actualization of the religious and moral imperative. For this, the Muslim is ever so grateful. Ambiguity and error have been man's most pernicious religious enemies. God has always been known by man, from Adam down. He has always recognized something he called "religion" or "morality," an "ought" which he regarded worthy of actualizing and being. But ever did he stumble and struggle and miss the exact application of this divine ought to ease his day to day problems!

Islam holds that in His mercy, God sent a prophet to each and every people, that all prophets have taught essentially the same lesson. Assuming that God cannot be subject to change, His will, the content of all revelations, must therefore be the same. It is not becoming of a God, if He is Almighty, Omniscient, as well as Transcendent that His will for man would change from place to place or age to age. Certainly, the means of obedience by man may and did change, but not that to which man's obedience is the response, namely the divine commandment.

This notwithstanding, there is a sense in which the divine commandment itself may have changed. That is the condition where the commandment is not a categorical imperative of goodness, justice or charity but a prescription of how in any species of concrete cases, goodness, justice or charity may be realized. Prescriptive religious laws do indeed change; for they are dependent upon the concrete situations where they are to apply. But that is a change in the accidents of revelation, not in the substance. Before Muhammad, revelation consisted of both the substance of divine will which includes the values, and the accidents which consist of the prescriptive legislations determined by the relativities of history. Islam asserts that the substance of all past revelations is the same, and it bases its claim on the inconsistency of divine transcendence with change. It recognizes the requisites of history as demanding change but as affecting only the "how" of religion, never the "what." The succession of past prophets Islam explains as necessitated either by changing situations or by aberration and misunderstanding of the substance of revelation.

Muhammad, therefore, is not claimed by Muslims to have brought anything new to the revelations of past prophets. His revelation is a confirmation of all previous revelations. Moreover, the revelation to Muhammad, the Qur'an, is imperishable because God declared Himself its protector and guardian. Hence the Muslims responded by committing it to memory by millions of persons across the centuries so that it is not possible for it ever to disappear from the earth. They have frozen the Arabic language, with all its grammar, syntax and lexicography that an understanding of the language of revelation may forever be possible and easy.

But isn't the Qur'an subject to the change affecting all prescriptive legislations? Muslims hold the Qur'an to be essentially a statement of religious ends, of the what of divine will. They do not deny that the Qur'an does include some legislation; but they hold that element to be of lesser importance than the rest. Out of a total of 6236 verses, hardly 500 are prescriptive, the rest being an exhortation to piety and virtue in general terms. They hold that God will not need to send another revelation, partly because He has placed in man's hand an imperishable and definitive statement of His will, viz., the Qur'an, and partly because He wishes man to discover and to elaborate the how's by which the will of God is henceforth to be realized. It is not by accident therefore that the Qur'anic revelation is not prescriptive in the main; it is so because the divine plan relegated law-making to man, as long as the principles and values of which the prescriptive laws are to be embodiments, are those which God had revealed.

Three important conclusions rest upon this position. First, there is no need for a prophet after Muhammad. That which necessitates the advent of another prophet – namely, corruption or loss of the revelation, or change of situations requiring a corresponding change in prescriptions – cannot come to pass. The Qur'an is imperishable; and prescriptive legislation is the duty and prerogative of men. Second, Muhammad is the last of the prophets, sent not to a people, but to the whole of mankind. As the archetypal adherent of the religion he received from God, Muhammad is the exemplar of Islam, whose Sunnah, or concrete example is normative.

Muhammad was not therefore merely the messenger who conveyed the message of his Lord *verbatim*. He concretized, particularized, specified, and made prescriptive the divine message. God had prepared him for the task, and his people never knew of a single flaw in his character. That is why God said in the Qur'an that in Muhammad's conduct stands *par excellence* the example for Muslim emulation. Two singular merits are therefore his by divine arrangement, namely, *verbatim* delivery of the message and its concretization in life. Both meanings are remembered, articulated *de novo*, and celebrated on his birthday.

On that day, as on every day but with yet more emphasis, the Muslim celebrates the advent of Muhammad. The Sunnah or example of Muhammad has been observed by him in so many events of every day. On this day, the Muslim is especially drawn to the realization of his need for this Sunnah, of the tremendous effort the Prophet's companions, their children, grandchildren and great grandchildren have exerted in keeping it pure and unadulterated, whether from well-meaning misinterpretation or unconsciously erratic conveyance. There was hardly any trouble in preserving and conveying the text of the Qur'an, as we have already seen. Its language and style are so radically different from the sayings of Muhammad or of any man that not much training is needed to distinguish the divine language from the human. But Muhammad's language is indeed human. Sifting the historically authentic traditions of the Prophet was a task demanding stupendous care.

For this task, the Muslims invented a number of disciplines. A number of them had to do with language. Assisted by the disciplines of grammar, syntax, lexicography, etymology and philology, redaction and literary aesthetics, all of which were designed primarily to help non-Arab, non-desert Muslims and all later generation Muslims to understand the Qur'anic text, the Muslims invented the disciplines of textual criticism, form-criticism, redaction-criticism, topical criticism and historical criticism to examine the texts of the hadiths. They devised and established other new disciplines, namely, biography, historiography and personal and social analysis, to investigate the truthfulness of the narrators of the hadith. They established canons of internal criticism for the former, and canons of external criticism for the latter.

Their job was not absolutely definitive, from the very nature of the case. Hence, they did not throw away what they found falling short of absolute authenticity, but satisfied themselves with categorizing it as such, reminding their reader that God knows better than they. Their researches enabled them to classify all the traditions of the Prophet's doing and saying according to their degree of authenticity in descending order. First are those which report a deed of the Prophet which he taught to the Muslims and the latter performed repeatedly ever since. This was an "actional" Sunnah which the Muslims believe is hardly capable of error, considering its universal, repeated and public nature. Second, came those hadiths of juridical nature which had visible and public consequences in history and had thus been verified by the incontrovertible facts of that history. Third came those hadiths of a religious or moral nature which are obviously consistent with the Qur'an and were thus meant to illustrate or exemplify its ideas and injunctions. Last were those hadiths which carry some creative, innovative direction, or tell something not reported by other known narratives or traditions.

The Muslim looks to the Prophet's Sunnah under these categories. He is careful to call the Prophet's exemplification canonized by the Qur'an itself *al-sunnah al-ṣaḥīḥah* (the verified Sunnah) thus keeping the door always open for the possibility of human error; indeed, for removing error from the precincts of the divine will which alone is religion, the imperative for man.

CHAPTER II

The Hijrah

IMPORTANT as the Prophet's birthday may be, it was not deemed by the Muslims to be the proper beginning for the Islamic calendar. It must be kept in mind that Muhammad was not the first prophet. Before him, a countless number of prophets have come and delivered the same message. True, they regard him to be the last, according to the divine description of him in the Qur'an as the "seal" or last of the prophets (Qur'an 33:40). The revelation he brought, like the preceding revelations, contains the same and whole content of the divine will. The *verbum dei* it conveyed is preserved intact and whole and its continued presence obviates the need for a new revelation. God's will is immutable in its substance, it is not subject to the vicissitudes of change. This substance is the body of principles and values expressed in the Qur'an. Not only do Muslims amply fulfill the obligation to preserve the Qur'an in its totality, committed to memory, written in the most sublime calligraphy in the best specimens ever produced by the arts of book-making which it alone engendered, and daily recited from cover to cover by thousands and millions of people publicly around the globe, but God Himself promised to preserve it intact forever.

The advent of the Prophet is hence indicative of a contact with divinity which brought to mankind knowledge of His will. It also indicates the preparation of this will for implementation through exemplification by the Prophet. As such, the whole significance of the advent is a matter for the divine economy, not the human. It does not necessarily include the commencement of the Islamic movement in history. The Islamic calendar had therefore to have another beginning.

It was ʿUmar ibn al-Khaṭṭāb, the second caliph (12-22 AH/634-644 CE) who established the Islamic calendar as beginning on the day of the Prophet's hijrah (July 16, 622 CE), i.e., his emigration to Madinah. The reasoning was precise and clear. Islam was not only a divine dispensation, nor one to be observed merely by man as an individual person, but one to constitute total guidance for the community, the state and world order. It is meant to be an ideology for a comprehensive movement issuing from Makkah and enveloping the earth and mankind. When did it launch itself on this cosmic career? Not on Muhammad's birthday! Nor on the first day of revelation when the Prophet himself was not yet quite sure of what was happening! Nor on the emigration of some of the Prophet's companions to Ethiopia, for their flight was one of refugees! But it launched itself on the emigration of the Prophet, or really the day after, when he proclaimed the establishment of the Islamic state and launched Islam as a world movement and a cosmic mission.

Was such a launching necessary for the religion itself? Was it not an accident of history, or a deliberate pursuit of men and hence a human *desideratum*?

No, answers the Muslim. Involvement in history was essential to Islam and its ultimate end. Islam taught that piety, spirituality, and religious felicity are vain and empty if they are meant for the subject alone. The point is clearly discernible in the realm of morals. It is possible to think of an ethic of intention where the good, or value, is defined in terms of the psychic states of the subject, i.e., of the determinants of his will in its personal moment. Such would be a subjective ethic whose ultimate judge on earth is the subject's own conscience, since only conscience penetrates to those inner layers of personal consciousness where the ultimate motives rest. Such, for instance, would be the opposite of an ethic of consequences, of a utilitarianism which defines the good, and hence the ethical merit of the deed, in terms of the external, obvious, measurable advantages in space and time which it engenders.

So with religion as such, in its totality, Islam is not a personalist, subjective religion like Christianity had been understood to be in the majority of cases over most of its twenty centuries of history. It is, rather, a mobilization of man to enter history, to interfere in its processes, to reorient its forces and therewith, men and nature, toward rekneading the cosmos and remolding it after the pattern God has revealed. The Muslim sees his vocation precisely in this: to enter history and therein to reshape the world.

Since nothing in creation is sacred, the sacred being alone God who is outside of creation, everything in creation is equally necessary, valuable and pertinent to the task once that is defined in terms of *Khilāfah* or vicegerency, of God. Those religions which bifurcated the world into sacred and profane, end up by dividing man's life accordingly. Under their view, religion is relevant on one day but not on the other; at worship in church or temple but not outside; during old age but not in youth; for personal acts but not for general economic and social behavior; for neighbor to neighbor conduct but not decisions and deeds of state.

All this is implicit in the Muslim's celebration of the hijrah. It is a reminder to him of another year past and another to begin. It is a moment of stocktaking, not in the domain of personal life, but in that of public life where the subject is Islam as world movement, as world state. How close is the world movement the Prophet had launched in Madinah to realizing its God-given objective? How far is it from including and mobilizing humanity? From transforming that humanity into monuments of genius, heroism and saintliness? From transforming nature into paradise?

CHAPTER 12

Isrā' and *Mi'rāj*

AS the youngest of the world religions, and as one born in the cradle of ancient civilizations, of Judaism and Christianity, Islam could not omit to relate itself to these religions. Its theory of prophecy already bound Islam to recognize the prophethood of the Hebrew prophets as well as of Jesus, whose memories were alive. The Qur'an mentions many of them, and pays particular attention to Abraham, Jacob, Shuayb, Moses, David, Solomon, Jonah, and Jesus. They and their followers it identifies as *ḥanīfs*, i.e., persons who were neither Jewish, nor Christian, nor adherents of Makkan religion, and yet were held in utmost respect for their moral uprightness, their religious vision and spirituality. Islam had therefore to specify its relation to them.

To begin with, it identified itself with the *ḥanīfs* whose head it identified with Abraham. The *ḥanīfs* were the Arab carriers of the whole legacy of Semitic religious consciousness, from Lipit-Ishtar to Sargon and Hammurabi, to Abraham and Moses and finally to Jesus. Undoubtedly their ranks were swelled by those refugees who ran away from persecution in Palestine, Jordan and Syria where the religious establishment was often in conflict over what was deemed to be ortho-dox Judaism and orthodox Christianity. The state religion of David, the post-exilic version canonized by Ezra and Nehemiah, the literal, legalistic version of the Pharisees, Maccabees and the Rabbinic

53

schools, all these did not become established without producing recurrent waves of dissidents some of whom found refuge among Arabs with some affinity to their own views. Likewise in Christianity, where the disagreements of the churches about Christology nearly always led to the banishment and/or persecution of some adherents. Mention should be made of Jewish refugees escaping the forced Hellenization of Alexander's heirs, and of the Christian refugees escaping Roman and Jewish persecution. This is also borne by the fact that "*ḥanīf*" is the Arabic form of the Aramaic *hanepai* which means heretic, rejected or separatist, which is exactly what such refugees would be from the religious establishment's point of view. But the *ḥanīfs* could not have all been such refugees. For it is impossible for any refugee of a different religion from the Arabs to choose to go to them for refuge, unless some Arabs were already of the same faith or sympathized therewith. The ranks of such native *ḥanīfs* may have been swelled by those emigrants who, in course of time, were naturalized and Arabized.

Islam's self-identification with the *ḥanīfs* was total. Ethnically, they regarded Abraham as their ancestor, and asserted him to be the first *ḥanīf*. The *ḥanīfs* had no known scripture, a fact which facilitated identification of Islam with them. With what was known of their religion among the Makkans, Islam agreed without reservations. This included monotheism, transcendence of the Godhead, universalism and a strict morality of chivalrous, pietistic and humanitarian values.

Judaism and Christianity were a different case. Each of them was a continuing establishment with its own scripture, its own *magisterium* and institutions. Something of their doctrines was perfectly true and genuine and hence agreeable to identify with. Other parts expressed views foreign to the whole Semitic tradition and were hence found to be in diametrical opposition to Islam. The Qur'anic criticism of these religions belonged to the Makkah period of revelation when Muslims had no relations with any people of different faith except the Makkans. Islam's criticism of the two religions is hence independent of the sociopolitical involvement of the Muslims with Jews and Christians. Islam was not shy to proclaim its continuity with both, its essential identity with both. It recognized them as legitimate religions whose ultimate source is God. But it criticized them mercilessly where their scriptures had been tampered with so as to contain men's fabrications alongside genuine revelation, and where it found their adherents' observance of the injunctions of the two religions deficient or wanting. In so doing, Islam achieved two goals: It related itself to these religions as members of one family whose source is one and the same God; and it distinguished itself from their human distortions by inviting their own adherents to exercise their common sense and do some Old Testament and New Testament criticism.

The *Isrā'-Miʿrāj* celebrates this discovery by Islam of itself as one with Judaism and Christianity, represented by the story of Jerusalem which the Prophet has visited miraculously in a single night's journey, and by his discourse with the prophets of God when he was lifted from Jerusalem to heaven on that same night. Obviously, a night journey to any distant city would have been equally miraculous. Heaven could, on the other hand, be reached from any locality on earth. Why then was Jerusalem chosen? Evidently because that city was the religious capital of Judaism and Christianity, and the abode of the prophets, with which Islam sought to identify itself. Already, the Muslims were turning North to Jerusalem in prayer.

The tradition has brought down the details of the event as told by the Prophet. He was awakened at night by the angel who on many earlier occasions had brought down the revelation to him. The angel brought to him a special steed which he mounted. The steed then flew across space, not without enabling the Prophet to recognize the travelers on the road and their caravans. Once in Jerusalem, the Prophet tethered his steed to the "wailing wall" adjoining *al-Aqsa* and from the rock now under "the Dome of the Rock" ascended to heaven where he led all the prophets assembled to meet him, in prayer and praise to God. God instructed His Prophet to institute salah in Islam. He was then taken on a tour of heaven and hell, Muslim reports of which have become the source for many romantic and speculative accounts of Heaven in Islam and the West. We should note here that Dante's *Divina Comedia* was a Christian adaptation of this Muslim theme.

In celebrating *al-Isrā'* and *al-Miʿrāj* Muslims celebrate the great unity of all the prophets, and consequently, of all the religions, notably those associated with Jerusalem and the surrounding countryside. A very special place among the prophets is accorded to Abraham, Moses and Jesus, founders of the three main streams of the Semitic family of religions.

Part IV

The Muslim Family

CHAPTER 13

Woman

WOMAN, in Islam, was created by God to be man's partner. The Creator built into both man and woman a mutual correspondence so that each would find quiescence and contentment in the other. The Qur'an calls man and woman a "garment" for each other signifying their reciprocal closeness to each other (Qur'an 2:187 – what is physically and continuously closer to oneself than one's clothing?), and their mutual interdependence. As far as religious duties are concerned, Islam made the sexes absolutely equal. It has exempted her from these duties when she is menstruating, pregnant or recovering from giving birth to a child. For the first time in human history, woman was granted by God an incontrovertible and autonomous legal personality, and complete civil rights. The highest aspiration of women's liberation movements has been achieved in Islam by 625 CE.

As a complete legal person the adult woman is granted title by Islam to keep her name forever; to have, to keep and to sell movable and immovable property as she pleases in perfect freedom. Her deliberate consent has to be sought for any transaction involving her, be it the least of her property, the cultivation of her field, or, above all, her marriage. She could not be coerced into anything. Unless she was a minor, and hence dependent upon her parents and guardians, or she has appointed another person to be her attorney–at–law or representative, she has to exercise her rights in person in order for the transaction to be legally valid.

Woman, in Islam, is not the source of evil. She did not tempt Adam; nor did the devil, or death, whether physical or moral come to the world through her. The Qur'anic story of Adam and Eve does not even mention Eve in the act of disobedience. The disobedient act was not sexual; nor did it have anything to do with the "tree of knowledge." Pursuit of knowledge is in Islam a paramount duty, not an evil. The Qur'an does say that both Adam and Eve were chased out of Paradise; but it adds that they repented and that God had forgiven them. Hence, there is no "fall" in Islam, and no resultant "original sin" in any form. St. Paul's condemnation of woman as the vehicle through which death came into the world, whether physical or moral, is totally absent in Islam.

Woman, therefore, is innocent. She is a positive good, a consoler, a source of happiness and fulfillment to man, as man is to her. For Muslims sex is no problem at all; it is natural like food and drink, growth and death. It is God-created, God-blessed, God-instituted. It is not ridden with guilt; but, like woman herself, innocent. Indeed, sex is highly desirable. The Qur'an has prohibited celibacy for His sake, and the Prophet has ennobled marriage by making it his Sunnah, or example, and hence normative for every Muslim male and female. Like everything else pertinent to life on earth, Islam made sexual gratification of men and women a piece of piety, of virtue and felicity.

Since woman is no more a chattel but a full legal personality, sexual intercourse with her cannot be a random affair but must be done, first with her consent, and second in responsibility. The latter does not fall only upon man, but upon woman as well. Sexual promiscuity is condemned vehemently because, by definition, it is a violation of responsibility by either party.

Man-Woman relations have to be ordered and governed if the ethical demand of responsibility is to be met. To this end, Islam provided a whole system of laws governing those relations; for it believes that man-woman affairs cannot be left to the whim of the moment, nor to the arrangements of others, as in the case of minors where sex is irrelevant since it is an adult affair. Marriage itself, as an institution, is regarded by Islam as nothing but a solemn compliance with the ethical requisite of responsibility. If it condemns a sexual act outside of marriage as a punishable crime, it does not do so of the sexual act in itself, but of the act as violation of responsibility.

It may be difficult to see why Islam regards sexual intercourse between unmarried consenting adults as irresponsible. The fury and flamboyance of passion may well blind the person to responsibility. A cooler presence of mind, however, always reveals that in man-woman relations there is a physical side, an emotional side, as well as a spiritual side; that adulterous connections are fulfillment in only one of these sides, especially the physical; but that it is often entered into at the cost of the long run emotional side, and always at the cost of the spiritual. For the partner in adultery is precisely the person who is using the other, or allowing himself/herself to be used, as an object. Where a partner regards his or her person as well as the other person as an end, surely he or she should be willing to transform the relation into marriage. For marriage in Islam is a civil contract, not a sacrament, by which the partners proclaim their plan in freedom and responsibility, henceforth to regard each other as ends, and not as means. Let us then turn to the laws of marriage.

CHAPTER 14

Marriage

MARRIAGE in Islam is not a sacrament. It is not a bond made in heaven, but right here on earth. Like all human bonds it is dissoluble. It is a pledge or contract by which the partners regulate their mutual relations. Like any other contract, it has a few constituents, or necessary provisions. If these are satisfied, the contract may contain any other provisions the two partners agree to include therein. There must be two adults consenting in total freedom to marry each other. The minor may be married by his or her parents but he or she has the full right, upon reaching adulthood, to consummate the marriage contract or to reject it. Even if the marriage had already been consummated, Islam gives the right to either partner, upon reaching adulthood, to dissolve it if they wish.

The second requirement is that the contract contains specification of two dowries, both incumbent upon the male and payable to the female. The first is to be given and received before consummation of the marriage. It usually consists of gifts of jewelry and clothing which become the woman's personal property, and henceforth inalienable without her consent. The second is hypothetical and falls due if and only if the marriage is terminated by divorce. Since divorce in Islam is possible for the male by repudiation, the second dowry acts as the female's "insurance policy" against irresponsible conduct of the male.

The third constituent of the Islamic marriage contract is the presence of two witnesses and their attestation to its contents or terms. The contract is not valid unless it is public, for when the responsible commitment is made before one's peers, it is more likely to be kept.

Besides these three constituents the parties to the contract can add other provisions they wish provided such do not violate the laws of morality. A marriage contract may stipulate the style of life to which man or woman is entitled. It can provide for this marriage to be monogamous by stipulating that it would terminate (and hence the second or deferred dowry would fall due) if the husband contracts another marriage.

Islam does permit divorce. Divorce can take place by solemn repudiation by the husband, but the law requires that such repudiation be made three times to be effective. It demands that after the first and second repudiations, marriage counselling and arbitration by near relatives or others nominated by the husband and wife deal with the dispute and restore domestic harmony. On the third repudiation, divorce becomes final, though God called it "most hateful." In order to prevent entering into it nonchalantly and irresponsibly by the husband, Islam decreed that no man may take back in marriage his wife whom he had divorced unless that woman had married another man and been divorced by him. Such marriage constitutes a terrible humiliation for both; and its scepter acts as a second deterrent, after the second dowry. A wife may divorce her husband by court decision, not by repudiation. In this case she would have to establish in court one of the legal reasons justifying divorce such as contagious sickness, prolonged absence, impotence, cruelty, adultery, etc. A divorce granted by the court is always final.

Islam also permits polygyny. A man may marry more than one wife. There are situations in personal human affairs where the best solution may well be a polygynous arrangement. And there may be situations in human society with an excess of women over men, where widowed or divorced women, oft with child and devoid of support, would find polygynous arrangements far more conducive to happiness than fending on their own. The plural marriages of the Prophet in Madinah, after the death of his first wife who gave him all his children and kept him happy for over a quarter of a century, were of this kind. A refugee widow with five children whom nobody wanted, a divorced wife of a former slave whom everybody was too proud to approach, an old matron whose relatives the Prophet wanted to reconcile, etc. – such were the women he married in his later life. Having given woman full legal personality and all civil rights, having endowed her with the full freedom to dictate the terms of her marriage, and having provided her with an "insurance policy" against divorce whose "blank lines" she alone would fill, Islam may well be called the best "friend" woman ever had.

Beside these legal provisions, Islam prescribed a whole range of ethical directives. Women are to be treated with love and kindness, for they are a gift from God. To them belong all rights in the same measure as duties are incumbent upon them. They are to keep their chastity, to run their homes, and with their husbands, to implement the highest injunctions of Islamic society and state.

CHAPTER 15

The Extended Family

IT is quite possible that some women may not incline towards married life and happiness as envisaged by Islam. Some women have a penchant for different kinds of career, for art, science or some productivity other than is usually associated with married home life. This need is not new. It did not start with the industrial revolution which extricated woman from her home to work in office and factory. The need is as old as humanity, and has raised problems before women's careers took them outside their homes. However, the problem is more often than not that the career-bound woman wants to have both marriage, home and children as well as a career, and finds the two irreconcilable.

To relieve woman from having to have a career in order to provide for herself, Islam prescribed support for woman whether minor or adult, by her nearest male relative on equal level as his own. This prescription is not suspended except when she marries. Then, her support falls upon her husband. When divorced or widowed, the prescription still holds, except when she is pregnant or nursing a child. In that case, her "husband" is obliged by law to support her and her child for two years after childbirth. Since she is this well provided for all the length of her life, Islam prescribed that woman would inherit only half the share of the male.

Nonetheless, there are women for whom even this economic guarantee is not sufficient. Some women are creative and their creativity may well demand external occupation for self-fulfillment. If she is the sole female adult living in a cellular family, either her career or her home has to bear the cost. One of the two has to give in. Otherwise, she can have both only in succession, children and home in the early period of her married life, and career in the later period. But long absence from the period of learning and advanced age might have already ruined her chances for a great creative career. In this case, she would more likely be able to do supportive service as a secretary, assistant, sales clerk or factory hand. If she were to take up her career in her prime age, the children would have to suffer; and so would the happiness of the home. Home is not only a bedroom and a kitchen. To fulfill themselves, humans need beauty, a measure of home-leisure where beauty of ambiance combines with friendly converse and pleasant activity. This is not likely to be available in homes where both parents are out working. Such parents would not be prepared to give each other the quiescence needed by each of them.

It would be otherwise if the home also contained other adult males and females, if it were an "extended family" home. Parents, sisters and brothers, grandparents, uncles and aunts, would give the home of the career-woman all the care it needs without her having to feel a wit obliged or superfluous. For the home equally belongs to all. If she has a child, the love and attention the relatives give is a blessing because of the blood-relation. This does not necessarily prevent her from putting her own touch to her quarters or to the home as a whole, nor from taking her children into her own motherly care after her work hours. The point is that in her absence, the house is not left unattended, or attended by foreign servants; and the children are not left to the internet, television set, the foreign babysitter or the "day-care center."

Moreover, the variety of characters and personalities, of moods and temperaments in the extended family home, provides for everybody the opportunity to do what he pleases in company of those who love him most. Be his or her mood one of joy and merrymaking, of despondency and crying, of friendly converse or meditation, of hard work or rest, of an outdoor promenade or a close *tete-a-tete*, husband, wife, son or daughter would nearly always find someone in the extended family to join him or her in that activity. If the mood is one of isolation and withdrawal, that too is permitted without offense or guilt, for the people in question are one's beloved, one's near relatives. Such company is absolutely essential for personal sanity and social health. Humans need love, counsel, company and altruistic concern as much as they need food and air. Total privacy can be obtained only at the cost of loneliness and is unworthy of it. The consequences of loneliness far outweigh the satisfaction which privacy sometimes furnishes.

Not only does the extended family make careers outside the home, as well as inside when the career is executed at home, possible but it makes the whole of society healthier. The extended family is the best guarantee against psychic ills and aberrations of all sorts. Islam has not only recommended it as good. It has buttressed it with laws. Every human in need, it prescribed, is entitled to the support of his nearest relative. In complement of this it prescribed that a person's legal heirs are not only one's spouse and children, but vertically in both directions, all his living parents and grandparents, and all his grandchildren and their children. All these members of the family are hence kept together by love as well as by law.

Part V

The Muslim Worker

CHAPTER 16

Stewardship of Nature

IT has been said earlier that man was created to be God's *khalīfah* or vicegerent on earth; that this means that he is expected to transform the world from what it is into what it ought to be. We also said that the will of God in nature is being fulfilled necessarily through the workings of natural law. Finally, let us remember that in the Qur'an, God declared everything in creation is designed and/or redesignable to serve man's happiness and lead to his felicity.

From this it follows that nature is not an enemy. It is not a demonic force challenging man and inciting him to conquer and subdue it. Such a view belongs to those religions whose cosmogonies make the world itself a god, whether good or bad and more often the latter. Such gods, or chthonic forces, must be appeased, if not subdued or manipulated so as to work for man's advantage. Islam regards nature as inert and neutral, a great positive blessing at best, whose joys are advance payments on the rewards of Paradise. It is an orderly cosmos created by God as the theater where man is to do his good deeds, perfectly fitted and equipped by the Creator according to the best measurement, the best form, the best pattern, and is hence absolutely free of any flaws.

In nature, happenings take place in accordance with natural laws, i.e., with the will of God. Hence, it is orderly. But its orderliness depends upon its Creator whose will it follows. This will is not whimsical; the Qur'an describes it as eternal and immutable. Hence, causal determination in nature may well be trusted to function. This trust which is the base of nature's orderliness is a function of man's vicegerency. For if man is to perform in nature, the system would have to be trustworthy, capable of receiving man's efficacious interference for the production of given and predictable results. Otherwise, if human causal efficacy could not be trusted to produce the predicted results, then purposiveness is destroyed and with it, the divine assignment of vicegerency.

Muslims have looked upon nature, following these principles, as an open book, a second revelation from God, which anybody could read who has cultivated the requisite knowledge and discipline. The Qur'an, they maintained is easier to read. Its statement of the will of God is direct and eloquent. Nature, on the other hand has to be "treated" to uncover her secret, her law, by scientific investigation and experimentation. But with some preparation, its truth is as public as that of the Qur'an.

This explains why the Arabs of the Arabian Peninsula, who had never developed any science to mention, fell upon the scientific legacy of classical antiquity with such enthusiasm that around 700 CE, a chemistry or botany manuscript would be travelled for from Eastern Persia to Alexandria, and would be gladly exchanged for a thousand golden pieces. By 800 CE, however, there remained nothing of the scientific and philosophical achievements of antiquity but was well known and mastered by the Muslims. Gradually, this led to the presuppositions of Greek natural science which were found to conflict with the Islamic notion of God.

The problem was not the concern of the scientists who continued with their work unconcerned with those deeper issues. The philosophers took up the problem and, in their hands, the vague assumptions were clarified and pushed to their ultimate conclusions. Cosmic order became cosmic determinism, matter became eternal, divine initiative and providence were denied. The Aristotelian categories were the seemingly irrefutable base. If natural law is truly law, its application must be universal. This gives us a closed cosmos where everything cannot happen except by a cause sufficient to bring it about. But if such a cause is there, its effect must necessarily follow. Thus, the chain of causality envelops the world. God may have built up the system; but does not run it. Like clockwork, it runs itself. Matter, the presupposition of everything, cannot be destroyed. It only changes form. Hence, it cannot come into being i.e., be created. It is eternal, coeternal with God.

It was the great al-Ghazālī who dealt the death blow to this kind of philosophy. Like David Hume who followed him almost a thousand years later, al-Ghazālī analyzed the causal connection and found it implying no necessity. That A follows *after* B, he reasoned, which is all that the observations of science establish, does not necessarily mean or imply that A happens *by* B. The judgment "*B* is the cause of A" is only a generalization of probable validity, a validity growing in probability the more often we experience A following upon B but never reaching a perfect validity of I. If the scientist is absolutely certain that A will follow upon B, whence then does his assurance come? It is his faith that the world order, or ontological equilibrium which brought about the last instance of the claim, will not fail to operate in the future. This faith is the product of religion, not science. Matter may have been at the base of all events and even antedate them. But it could not have brought itself into being. If it has a cause, its cause could not be caused in turn, if an infinite regress is to be avoided. Modern astronomy and space science are not opposed to the doctrine of an expanding universe. This conclusion is equally that of contemporary philosophy of science, the closed cosmos theory being a nineteenth century fad which the twentieth century has exploded.

Nature, we may conclude, is pliable and capable of change. Man is capable to steward its forms to what ought to be. Agriculture, horticulture, engineering and architecture, in short, civilization itself consists precisely in such stewardship. But no alteration performed in vengeance or resentment against nature or without responsibility to the Creator of nature, can remain innocent for long. For if nature is not used as a gift from God given for a moral purpose, its abuse is certain. If the moral purpose of God is denied, may it not be abused? Raped, as modern man has done? In Islam, no such souring of the quest or usufruct of nature is possible. For, for the Muslim, the secret working of nature is God's pattern and will; and the utility of nature is a divine gift meant solely for fulfillment of the moral law.

CHAPTER 17

Wealth

THERE is no limit in Islam to man's usufruct of nature except the limits of the moral law. This law prohibits such use of nature as may hurt the neighbor which the universalism of Islam identifies with all men present and future. Within the limits of this requirement, man may draw from nature as much as he desires. This means that Islam favors a market system where the combined forces of nature, of human labor, and accumulated science and wealth may be used to the full possible extent without harm to the others. Islam is definitely anti-poverty, which it declares to be the work of the devil. Man is responsible for his poverty, though when he suffers from poverty he is worthy of compassion and charity.

The Puritans believed that a sign of God's pleasure with a person is the good fortune He grants to him. They subscribed to a deterministic view of life, of nature and salvation. God is the decision maker. When He chooses to be pleased with him, He manipulates good material fortune to become his. Despite this divine pre-determinism, Puritanism succeeded in inciting quite an economic revival in America. Anxious to appear blessed, i.e., as a man with whom God is pleased, the Puritan over-exerted himself to become rich and succeeded in winning both wealth and, supposedly, the divine blessing. For he believed in the Puritan doctrine. Seeing himself prospering, his faith encouraged him to press harder, and the more he exerted himself and produced, the more he succeeded. The Muslim shared this belief and strengthened it with the faith that man stands obliged to remold nature and the world, if the meaning of his vicegerency is to be fulfilled. He understood God as commanding him to produce wealth that he and others may live and prosper. He thanked God if his effort succeeded and he bore in patience if it failed, holding his success and failure not necessarily, i.e., totally and exclusively related, to his effort. He held the decision of God and the result achieved on earth in inverse relation. If he succeeds, and he must do so on his own, God would reward him further. If he does not, he has only himself to blame, not God.

Every Muslim then desires and plans to become a "millionaire" if he takes his Islam seriously. Islam, however, warns him, that in amassing his wealth, he should earn it. He should not cheat his fellow humans of their wealth, but should produce his own. Islam prohibits gambling because it is a game of chance and its wealth, if it brings any, is not the result of effort and productive self-exertion. It constitutes no increase to the wealth of mankind. It urges man to produce new wealth, and holds the "self-made" man in special honor. The acrobatics of modern advertizing and the false enticements to buy the products of industry, to create new unnecessary needs for the new products coming out like a stream, and the planned short obsoletization of all things in order to keep the machines of industry running, are not acceptable to Islam. Other ways, more constructive and less consumptive, more universal in their distribution of products would have to be found.

Islam is against the hoarding of wealth. To discourage it, it has instituted the zakah, which if consistently applied to a hoarded wealth, would "eat it up" in one generation, the years needed for a tax of 2.5 per cent to exhaust the stationary capital. Such wealth ought to be in production, i.e., invested in productive undertakings which increase the general wealth of mankind, in enterprises which provide jobs for more people and bring the earth closer to paradise. To ply wealth back into production is one of the good effects of zakah. To insure this fructification of wealth and hence more employment and more production of real wealth, i.e., of goods and services, Islam prohibits interest.

Interest implies the accumulation of profit without taking risk, this being carried entirely by the borrower. In a sense, the lender too is commonly said to take a risk in lending his money. The fact is, however, that firstly, on the average his wealth is increasing despite a low rate of "bad debts." Otherwise no banker will stay in business for long. Secondly, the lender's risk is more often one of "easy" against "difficult" collection for he must have exacted from the borrower all the collateral and guarantees he possibly could. Islam seeks to eliminate the class of "financier" by goading the money-lender to invest his wealth in production directly. Islam would certainly bless the effort of any group of people who form a cooperative credit and thrift society whose purpose is to store the savings of members and lend money to the needy among them *without interest*, and according to the best judgment of his peers.

Once wealth is produced and appropriated, Islam requires that it be earned again, this time morally. It prescribes the zakah, or "sweetening" which once paid to society, makes the wealth in question *ḥalāl* or "sweet," now fully appropriable and investible by its owner in any way he wishes. It urges him to give more, this time at no fixed rate or time and to any one he pleases whom he thinks to be in need. This is called *ṣadaqah*. Unlike zakah, it is voluntary and may legitimately be whimsical. By instituting it, Islam sought to give the wealthy the means of making his love-of-neighbor effective in his own immediate vicinity, among his entourage.

Islam is against all "customs." This institution means building a wall or barrier against the free distribution of wealth around the globe. It means planting within the country a protected industry or agriculture for which it is not suited, in a kind of "hot-house" condition. A free world-wide distribution of wealth and goods, however, would not be effective without a free world distribution of labor. Indeed, Islam wishes for all "customs" and "immigration" institutions to disappear. Men and women ought to be free to live and work wherever they wish without checks, lets or hindrances. They should mix freely with one another, intermarry with and learn from one another. The best argument will naturally win the ensuing battle for the minds of men; and the better deeds will eventually win for their doer the leadership he deserves.

Part VI

The Islamic World Order

CHAPTER 18

The Universal Brotherhood
Under the Law

PERHAPS the greatest implication of Islam's confession that there is no God but God (with its tacit assumption that every man has been endowed by God with natural religion) is its universalism. All men, in its view, are God's vicegerents on earth. All are subjects under moral obligation and all are objects of one another's moral action. Obviously, the greatest threat to this universalism, and hence to Islam, is parochialism or provincialism, the view that some people are to value their distinction from the rest of mankind more than their communion.

That humans do in fact differ from one another is a platitude. There are kinds of differences. Some are natural, like color, shape, tallness and complexion. Others are natural but may be changed at will, such as weight and appearance, language and many customs. Others, like intelligence, vision, smell, taste and memory may be cultivable but less amenable to deliberate change. Undeniable as all these differences may be, the point Islam wishes to make is that they are irrelevant for measuring man's worth, for planning and organizing his societal activity and life. Man's creatureliness before God, the ultimate base uniting him with mankind, is far more important. To hold the opposite is to divide mankind into separate ethnic entities and to invite ethnic egocentrism, or nationalism, the view that limits man's love and care to members of his ethnic group, and allows that the good may be denied or even taken away from the outsider to the benefit of the insider. Ethnocentrism can also be purely separatist and isolationist, basing itself on negating the relevance of the outsider to anything pertinent to the ethnic group, whether the outsider is dying of hunger and injustice, or overflowing with culture and prosperity.

That charity begins at home is not denied by Islam. Nor is this principle all there is to ethnocentrism. The latter, like all varieties of nationalism, asserts that the ethnic or national group constitutes the limits of goodness, of the obligation to all instituted bodies to bring about well being and prosperity. Indeed, it even asserts the superiority of the ethnic group above all others and tolerates, on the basis of that superiority, taking away from all others to give to its own group. From the Islamic point of view, this is condemnable aberration. Agreeing with the principle of priority to the next of kin, Islam insists on defining the good in terms of the wellbeing of *all* human beings; on planning and organizing societal life and endeavor on *universalistic* basis.

Indeed, in ethnocentrism, Islam recognizes something of a sinister nature. This is not so much the action of ethnocentrism which can nearly always be justified on the basis of "charity begins at home," but the avowed base on which it rests its case. That its people are "the master race," "sons of God," the "chosen of God" while others are "the subject races," "sons of the devil," "of other inferior gods," or simply the creatures of the same God to whom they are not related in the same relationship as "His sons" or "His chosen," is not only false doctrine. It is sinister because of the deadening effect it has on man's awareness of his creatureliness before God which he shares with all mankind, because of its stilling effect on man's will to act on behalf of mankind. It is also sinister on account of the view of God and His creatorship it assumes. Under its view, either there are more than one God with two different creations, one superior the other inferior; or one God created two creations that one may lord it over the other. The former view is polytheistic; the latter is contrary to God's justice and ultimately, to His transcendence.

Islamic universalism holds all human beings to be entitled by nature to full membership of any human corporate body. For every one is at once subject and object of the one and same moral law. The unity of God is inseparable from the unity of His will which is the moral law. Under this one law, Islam seeks to rally the whole of mankind on equal terms. It does not have nor tolerates any one to hold a doctrine of election. Nobody, it asserts, has been predestined to any station. Such would contradict the moral nature of man and the divine plan which is the purpose of creation, namely, that man – every man – may fulfill the moral law and achieve felicity. Nor does Islam approve of any "doctrine of the remnant" which affirms that although some or most of the members of an ethnic group may do wrong, go astray or fall off from the state of election, there will always be a remnant that will not, and thus, will justify the ethnic group remaining the elect it claims to be.

This universalism of Islam does not preclude it from differentiating between human beings on the basis of their moral endeavor and achievement. Such would be equally contrary to the moral law which assigns "height" or "moral worth" in direct proportion to men's moral accomplishment. Indeed, such discrimination is not only well founded and tolerable, it is obligatory. This is what it means to honor the man of knowledge above the ignorant, the wise above the foolish, the virtuous above the vicious, the pious above the atheist or rebel, the just, loving and merciful neighbor above the unjust, hating, resentful, etc. Such discrimination is not only legitimate; it has the positive quality of contributing to general moral felicity by enticing men to excel in the deed. To excel in the deed is the purpose of creation itself. It is all that matters.

CHAPTER 19

The Islamic State and the *Pax Islamica*

WESTERN political theory defines the state as consisting of four elements: territory, people with common features, government, and sovereignty. It cannot be without territory, nor with an indefinite, boundless one. It cannot be universal, or include people without common features such as racial characteristics, language, customs and history. Finally, it must have corporate institutions and a government which together exercise sovereignty, i.e., enforce in all aspects of life one will which is assumed to be the single will of the whole. This is a definition of the western national state which is the creation of the last four to five centuries of western history.

Such western state is radically different from the Islamic state. The latter does have a territory but this is not essential. It can exist without it, as well as with one devoid of definite boundaries. Indeed the territory of the Islamic state is the whole earth, or better, the whole cosmos since the possibility of space travel is not too remote from us. Part of the earth may be under direct rule of the Islamic state and the rest may yet have to be included; the Islamic state exists and functions regardless. Indeed, its territory is ever-expansive. So is its people or "citizenry." For its aim is to include mankind. If it is at any time restricted to a few of the world's population, it does not matter as long as it wills to comprehend mankind. Its citizenry as we shall have occasion to see, need not be all Muslim. It has hardly ever been the case that all citizens of any Islamic state are all Muslims. What is important is that the citizenry includes all those humans who agree to live under its auspices because they approve of its order and policies. The Islamic state never binds anyone to its citizenship against his will. He is always free to move out, together with all his people, relatives, dependents and everything they possess.

The Islamic state derives its constitution from the Covenant of Madinah which the Prophet granted to the city upon his emigration thither in 622 CE. The spirit of that covenant determined every Islamic state in history. It provided that the Muslims, regardless of their origins, (they belonged to different tribes and nations) are one Ummah. That is to say, they constitute one corporate entity regulated by Islamic law. It has its own institutions, courts of law, schools for the education of its children, in contradistinction from all others. The Ummah's governance with a view to self-realization, to the full measure of its religion, its genius, its laws, its ethic and culture, is guaranteed. So is its perpetuity. For an Ummah ought to have the freedom to pass on to its offspring its legacy of religion and culture whole, if not enriched. The Ummah, then, by definition, is a community living up to its own ideals, or at least seeking to do so in perfect freedom.

Besides recognizing and establishing the Muslims as an Ummah, and hence wiping out their racial and tribal differences with the universalism of Islam, the Covenant of Madinah recognized and established the Jews as another Ummah, on equal par with the Muslim Ummah. They too constitute a community that ought to be given full freedom to realize itself according to its own legacy and genius. It should have its religion, social institutions, its own laws and courts to administer them, its own language and culture, its own ambiance and schools in which to bring up its children according to its own genius. It should enjoy all that is necessary to perpetuate itself.

A few years later, in 630 CE, the Christians of Arabia came to Madinah to negotiate their status with the Prophet. The Prophet received their delegation with open arms. He also allowed them to pray their prayer in his mosque. He presented them with Islam and argued with them for three days while they enjoyed his hospitality as was customary with the Arabs. Some were convinced, became Muslims and were immediately admitted into the brotherhood of believers as equals of all other Muslims. They became members of the Muslim Ummah. The others were not convinced and remained Christians. But they did choose to enter the Islamic state as citizens. Accordingly, they were granted the same status as the Jews and the Muslims. Henceforth they were to be an Ummah, on a par with the rest, enjoying the privilege of living as Christians in fulfillment of their legacy of religion and culture and of their will to perpetuity. They did not live in Madinah, like the Jews, but far away, in lands separated from Madinah. Just the same, the Prophet included them, thus expanding the jurisdiction of the Islamic state, and sent with them one of his trusted companions to be his representative in their territory. From that moment on, their protection from foreign aggression as well as from internal subversion fell to the Islamic state. It was the guarantor of their freedom, of their Christianness and of their self-continuation in history.

By the same logic, the Persian Zoroastrians, the Indian Hindus and Buddhists were included in the Islamic state as Ummahs on a par with the other Ummahs of Muslims, Jews and Christians. The Islamic state was their guarantor and protector whose duty is defined by its own constitution as enabling each to live in accordance with its own religion, ethic and culture, to perpetuate itself through the generations, in perfect freedom. The Islamic state is then not an exclusively Muslim state, but a federation of Ummahs of different religions and cultures and traditions, committed to live harmoniously and in peace with one another.

Islam, however, is a missionary religion *par excellence*. How then is this federal system accepted as a *modus vivendi* between Muslims and non-Muslims? Mission is certainly endemic to Islam. It flows from its essence as a universal religion. Every Muslim wishes that Islam would be the conscious religion of every man, as he realizes that it is the unconscious religion of every man which nurture and history has altered into something else. Islam also holds mission to be a duty incumbent upon every Muslim man and woman. This missionary spirit, or *daʿwah* (literally "calling" men to Islam) is not contradictory to the Islamic state. It is its ultimate objective. Within the Islamic state, as outside of it, therefore Muslims must carry out the mission. A verse of the Qur'an[1] assigns the duty to Muhammad *vis-à-vis* the Arabs, the first Ummah, and to the Ummah *vis-à-vis* the other Ummahs within the Islamic state. By logical extension, Muslims including their Prophet, have understood the Islamic state to be assigned the same duty *vis-à-vis* the other states.

The principle which makes all this possible without contradicting anything we have so far said is that of personal freedom. Under Islam, religious conviction is an entirely personal affair. Every man is free to convince and to be convinced. Unless and until he is convinced of the Islamic claim, he is perfectly entitled to be what he is and to continue to do so from generation to generation. The Muslim, therefore, may continue to missionarize, but he cannot coerce. Coercion (*ikrāh*), or subversion (*fitnah*) are punishable criminal violations in Islam. The non-Muslim, like the Muslim himself, is entitled to the full practice of his faith. Nor is either of them entitled to so run his affairs, or the Ummah's, as to interfere with the religious and cultural life of the other. Either of these practices is based on ethnocentrism or cynicism or the superiority of one Ummah over the other. Internally, the Islamic state cannot tolerate any encroachment of one Ummah over another. Its duty is the same towards all, viz., to keep the peace, to run the public services, to defend the totality, and to protect the rights and privileges of the persons and their Ummahs which make it up.

Externally, the Islamic state is ideological; i.e., it does have a world purpose which it pursues with all power at its disposal. It approaches other states, tribes, peoples, nations or groups with the proposal for them to enter as an Ummah within the Islamic state. Such entrance, it would explain, does not mean the entry of its people into the Islamic religion, nor any diminution, or even change, of any institution order or arrangement which has hitherto obtained within it. Nor does it mean any alteration of its economic arrangement, or the political sovereignty of its king, government, or governmental institutions. All these remain absolutely the same and will be guaranteed and protected.

---

1 Al Fārūqī is most likely referring to verse 2:143 of the Qur'an here, though he does not specify which verse he was actually referring to.

Its entrance into the Islamic state means only that its relations with that state will henceforth be relations of peace; that it is prepared to allow its citizens to hear and listen to the call of Islam while they call Muslims to anything they wish, if not to their own religion and worldview; in short, that neither will it wage war against, nor be waged war against by, the Islamic state, nor will it live in a state of *apartheid* from the rest of humanity.

The Islamic state is therefore not really a state but a world order, a *pax Islamica* with a government, a court, a constitution and an army, a sort of "United Nations" with "body" and "teeth." To enter it is to decide on peaceful intercourse with one's fellow-humans and to renounce war between the Ummahs once and for all. Evidently, not to enter it, to remain outside of it, is to assert the contrary; and hence to mean either national *apartheid* (isolation) or war and aggression. That is why Muslim theorists have called the Islamic state "the House of Peace," a real world-order or *pax Islamica*.

Force is not to be in the hands of any Ummah, not even the Muslim Ummah. It is to be used for putting down rebellion within any Ummah against its established institutions and authority; to restore to any Ummah any rights, privileges or properties which any other Ummah might have violated; and finally, to defend the world order itself against its enemies. No other use of power is legitimate. Truly, then, the world order Islam envisages is an ideal order of national and international relations, one which constitutes the only answer to the continuing malaise of the world situation. By comparison to it, a world peace based on atomic terror, on the balance of power or on the imperial tyranny of any Ummah over the others, is nothing short of Satanic.

The army of the Islamic state is Muslim since the duty of jihad or defensive war, is a religious duty falling on Muslims alone. Others may join if they wish to, in which case they would be exempted from the *jizyah*, and would be treated in exactly the same manner as Muslims. But they may not be conscripted by the government into military service. Their enlistment has to be entirely voluntary.

The Islamic state does not have to be a monolithic system where one and only one law, style of living, culture, religion and worldview obtain. This requirement has been relegated to the Ummah, and it is the latter which acculturates, integrates, and assimilates all elements into the Islamic unit and preserves its Islamic existence. Other Ummahs render the same services to their non-Islamic members. That is why the Islamic state can afford to be liberal and pluralistic. In fact, its constitution is the only one which enables it to be genuinely pluralistic, without attempt on its part to wipe out the differences between the Ummahs under the pretext of "national integration" and "national unity."

The task of acculturating and homogenizing its members fall to the Ummah, not to the Islamic state as such which must keep itself open to the possibility of other Ummahs doing the same to their own members. The Muslim Ummah within the Islamic state is indeed a monolithic entity governed by Islamic law. The citizen of the Islamic state is free to opt for any religion, for any Ummah within it. If he opts for an Ummah outside the Islamic state, he must emigrate thereto forthwith.

Finally, it should be noted that the Islamic state is an Islamic idea; that its men, energies and mind are all Muslim. Furthermore, it is a unique phenomenon on earth. History knows of no parallel to it. If similar states were to be formed by non-Muslims, this would be a welcome development. For the Islamic state can then feel certain that the day will not be distant when it can merge with the non-Islamic state since their constitutions are similar but their religions different. For it is essential to the constitutions of both states that they should seek to solve their differences in peace.

Part VII

Islamic Culture and History

CHAPTER 20

Islamic Culture

WE have seen in the foregoing chapter that it is upon the Ummah that the tasks of acculturating and Islamizing the members fall, as well as the preservation of their Islamicity. The system within the Ummah is quite monolithic, but with built-in mechanisms for creative self-renewal and reform. Islam is a comprehensive way of life. It is relevant for every aspect of life, for every deed. It is no wonder then that the Ummah would make itself felt in all walks of personal and public (corporate) life. Islam seeks to put itself in evidence in the style of life, at home, in the public building, on the street, in the institutions, the city — everywhere.

Islam teaches that God is indeed our Lord and Master. Consciousness of Him is the first and last requisite. For to know Him as God, i.e., as Creator, Lord and Master, as end of everything, is more than half the battle of existence and well being. To know God as God is to love and honor Him; it is to lay oneself open to determination by His will. For only that is *Islam* or submission. It is natural therefore that awareness of God be the objective of every endeavor; that the Muslim surround himself with all that reminds him of God; that within the Ummah, everything be theocentric, God-oriented.

Naturalism, or the perception of ultimate reality in nature, the assumption that nature is its own norm and measure, that the good, the true and the beautiful are in and of nature, is the antithesis of Islam. Islam resists taking nature for God and thus reducing His transcendence. Nature is the strongest contender for the place of God. Its position has been ever rising in the consciousness of western man since the Renaissance which in this sense, may be said to have dethroned God. Instead of God being the end and measure of all things, it installed man, as crown of nature; for he, it deemed, was the one destined to play the role of "measure unto all things."

This starting point gave the western and Islamic cultures their sense of beauty. For the Western Christian affected by the Renaissance, the beautiful is man. In man is exhausted the meaning of the sublime. The Christian doctrine of the incarnation through its idea of a God immanent in the flesh and hence in nature, eased the transfer from the Semitic notion of a transcendent God who is the absolute standard of beauty, truth and morality, to man as absolute standard. Henceforth the whole of Christian culture was to be transformed by this principle; just as Islamic culture remained true to the original Semitic vision that only God is God and hence, that only God is absolute norm, standard and measure of all things.

Beginning with the Renaissance, western man began to paint, carve and design in a way expressive of this naturalism. The Church fathers, custodians of the Christian vision, were shocked at first especially so by the representation of naked bodies; but they quickly acquiesced to this invasion of Western consciousness by pagan and naturalist Greece and Rome. This invasion was pervasive; not only in the visible arts but equally in all other aspects of culture. However, the various areas of culture were not all invaded at the same time. One could argue that in philosophy, it had to await the arrival of Descartes; in literature, the arrival of Erasmus; in music, that of Joseph Haydn.

The Muslims, on the other hand, developed the Arabesque, a design applicable to decoration as well as to architecture, to painting as well as to calligraphy, to town planning as well as to literature, to horticulture and aquaculture as to philosophy. The design is built on the laws of non-development, repetition, symmetry and momentum. The first means denial of nature whose law is certainly development, or movement from a state of genesis through successive states of growth and development ending in maturation, climax or consummation beyond which everything seems to be irrelevant to the natural process in question. Just as the Islamic view begins with a denial "No God but God," so does the universal patterns of Islamic art, language, thought and style begin with the negation of nature as measure and norm, as embodiment, locus, or carrier of the sublime.

The second principle on which the Arabesque is built is repetition and the third is symmetry. Nature is neither repetitious nor symmetrical. The leaves of the same tree may look alike; but each one is different from all the others. Likewise, the case with symmetry. The Arabesque denies naturalism through these principles, but that is not their only function. They are the elements out of which the Arabesque creates momentum or motion from one repeated pattern to another, *ad infinitum*. This is the fourth principle of the Arabesque. A row of bricks or a basket weave of threads or straws is both repetitious and symmetrical. The Arabesque arranges the symmetrically repeated elements or patterns in such a way as to generate motion, to pull the spectator from one unit in the design to the other and set him on a course which, from the very nature of the case, can never come to a natural conclusion. The work of art itself, the tableau, the facade, the story or the poem does come to an end, as it must. But the Arabesque or design in it never does. In graphic representation in a wall, a carpet, a miniature or a panel of wood or masonry, the Arabesque seems to continue beyond the natural limits of the object *ad infinitum*. The same is true of a composition of music or of poetry, where the elements and patterns differ, but not the design which never terminates when the performer or reciter stops, but creates a need to continue what has been experienced *ad infinitum*.

The purpose of developmental art is to arrest attention on the object developed which is directly or indirectly a human state or condition, and therein to contemplate its ultimacy or normativeness. This is true even in the still life or landscapes which are given not for themselves but for the human character or personality standing, as it were, behind them. The non-developmental character of the Arabesque aims at the opposite purpose. Not to arrest attention but, rather, to keep the pattern going in the imagination of the beholder, and, as it were, to carry the spectator by the momentum the rhythm of pattern has generated, outside the work of art presented, is to set consciousness on an infinite march which can never fulfill its end precisely because it has none. Here, an intuition is gained of the negative aspect of transcendent reality, namely, that it is infinite, never given to human sense perception, never graspable immanently in nature, and hence, never expressible. The Arabesque does not express God; but it does express sensibly and beautifully, the inexpressibility of God.

It is therefore not by accident that the Muslim surrounds himself with objects of art which all tell the same theme: "There is no God but God," whether discursively through calligraphy, or esthetically (i.e., as given to sense) through the Arabesque. His house, its facade, location, skyline, floor plan, interior and exterior decoration, all emphatically deny nature saying, as it were, nothing in nature is God or even a vehicle for God. Where they have been invested with Islamic beauty and hence, with Arabesque designs generating a momentum toward infinity, their expressiveness becomes all the more eloquent. What the Muslim loves to hear, likewise, be it instrumental or vocal music, the chanting of the Qur'an or the recitation of poetry, embody the same principles and express the same vision of the one transcendent God. Calligraphy, the supreme art of Islam, doubles its effect by adding to the sensory expression of infinity and inexpressibility of transcendent reality, by its Arabesque undulating patterns of lines and decoration, the direct discursive expression of God, His will and deeds, and man's place in the divine order of creation.

That is why the mosque, the supreme public expression of Islam, is an empty building, whose walls deny mass, weight, opaqueness and hence enclosure of space. Instead of enclosure, the mosque walls give the airy feeling of transparent screens of floating patterns which join the mosque to infinite space. The carpet which covers its floor, the capital which heads its pillar, the decorated panel into which all its surfaces are covered whether in wood, masonry, stucco or carved marble, the crenellated skyline – everything expresses the same theme of infinity and transcendence with one voice. Lastly, the bands, panels and rosettes of Arabic calligraphy reproducing verses from the Qur'an, as the chanting of the Qur'an usually reverberating between its walls, repeat the same theme explicitly and immediately.

Transcendence, or ultimate reality, namely Allah, touches every aspect of the Muslims life, as it pervades every product of his culture, as it dominates every corner of his consciousness. Both he and the modern western Christian are obsessed with great obsessions: the latter is obsessed with God-in-man, the Muslim is obsessed with God-in-God alone.

CHAPTER 21

Islamic History

ISLAM was born in Arabia. In a sense it had to. Being the crystallization of ancient Mesopotamian (Semitic) religion and wisdom, it could be reborn only in Arabia for two reasons. First, Arabia was the only corner of the ancient world which continued the legacy without falling under the influence of Egyptian, Greek and Zoroastrian culture. Whatever influence of this kind had reached Arabia was slight and in the periphery only, in Petra and Palmyra in the north, in Yemen in the south. The center remained unaffected.

Secondly, whatever was left of the Mesopotamian legacy in Arabia was assisted, bolstered and preserved not so much in the religious practices of the Pre-Islamic Arabs, but in their language and poetry. Here, their consciousness of transcendence was mirrored unconsciously. Their language was itself an Arabesque in its lexicography, syntax, grammar and literary esthetics. Their poetry was the *non plus ultra* of symmetry, repetition, non–development and momentum long before Islam. Nothing could have fitted the Islamic message better than the Arabic literary medium. Perfect correspondence between them is the inevitable conclusion of any student with the minimum perceptiveness. Nowhere else was any such consciousness mirrored in any language. When Islam came, it built its whole case on the literary sublime character of its revelations – the medium which the Arabs (and only the Arabs) could readily and perfectly appreciate. They knew what is and what is not miraculous or sublime in that medium. Even the enemies of Islam among the Makkans immediately recognized the *mysterium* in the revelation of Muhammad. Their vested interests and shock delayed them, but only for a very short while, in acclaiming it as divine.

Before the death of Muhammad, the whole of Arabia had acknowledged the new crystallization of its innermost, even unconscious, wisdom. It saw in Islam what Islam proclaimed itself to be, namely, that it is the quintessence of all ancient Semitic history, of all previous revelations and prophecies; that it is the thesis of transcendence, of a reality which Arab consciousness recognized as alone ultimate and truly transcendent. Arabia stood poised, now that Islam revealed to it its identity and destiny as the message-carrier of divine transcendence to the world.

Arabness, or this consciousness of transcendence mirrored in the Arabic language and poetry, had already penetrated to some degree the Fertile Crescent, its northern land bridge with Asia and Africa, before Islam. Indeed, the Fertile Crescent was Arabized in this sense by repeated migrations going back to Akkad in 3,000 BC or earlier. The later influences of the invading Philistines and "men of the mountains," of Hittites, Egyptians, Greeks and Persians, helped to confuse and veil, but not to extirpate or fundamentally alter, that consciousness. Arab transcendalist consciousness resisted the onslaught of Egyptianization, Persianization and Hellenization. They did so heroically in all that has come to us from the Pre-Islamic Fertile Crescent, whether it be language, works of art, law-codes, or literature. Scarred, their consciousness of transcendence certainly was, be they Christian, Jewish or Zoroastrian; but it was undaunted.

No sooner had Islam presented itself to them than they shed the confusion and dilution of ethnocentric Rabbinic Judaism, of trinitarian immanentist Christianity, of caste non-egalitarianism, and dualistic naturalism of Manichaean Zoroastrianism. They readily acknowledged Islam as their own, not as something foreign but as something they had always held but were somewhat unable to express so clearly as the Qur'an had done.

Within a generation, the ranks of Islam swelled to include the majorities of people in the temperate belt from the Atlantic to India. Thereafter, the conquests had come to a halt and the millions began the task of transforming the new vision of divine transcendence into visible civilization. The next four centuries saw the blossoming of Islamic culture and civilization throughout the lands. Every ethnic entity contributed its best, but under the transforming principles of Islam. Diversity there certainly were; but the overall unity was unmistakable.

First to develop were the sciences of language and *belles lettres*, the media of revelation. Determined by Islam, consciousness now demanded to be informed how Arabic language and letters acted as vehicles of transcendence. This was at the same time necessary for understanding the Qur'an, the word of God, by people who had not mastered the Arabic language as well as its people of the desert. Grammars, lexicographic and etymological dictionaries, syntactical analyses of all sorts, literary criticism and analysis of the Qur'an, of every poem, common saying or piece of oratory carried by memory, were written by the thousands, oft for the first time in the history of human culture and learning.

The religious vision of Islam was complete in the revelation, the Qur'an. That is why Islam does not have a religious history, that is a history of its formation as a religion. Such "history" is limited to the biography of the Prophet, the last 22 or so years of his life during which the revelation of the Qur'an was completed. Caught by this vision of Islam, the Muslims plunged themselves into implementation and concretization, into translating the normative principles of Islam into prescriptive directions for human conduct, in developing and establishing a viable methodology for such translation. It is here on this front that Islamic genius poured itself forth. In the realms of personal status, procedure, torts and contracts, international relations, crime and punishment, the Shariʿah, or Islamic law, remains to this day absolutely without parallel, and its bases in juristic thought unmatched.

Being avidly anxious to discover the will of God in nature, the Muslims quickly learned and assimilated the legacy of antiquity and moved far beyond it. Al-Bayrūnī measured the earth's perimeter within inches of the most exact measurements of our day; Ibn Sīnā's *Canon of*

Medicine and al-Rāzī's *Ad Almansorem* and *On Small Pox and Measles* remained the standard textbooks of the medical profession until the eighteenth century; Ibn al-Bayṭār's pharmacopia, *Simplicia*, was being printed in the main European languages as late as 1866. Arabic numerals moved arithmetic, and *al-Jabr* (Algebra) moved formal mathematics, to new realms of advance and achievement.

Everywhere the Qur'an was chanted in its original Arabic. Everywhere, its verses decorated every room and house and punctuated every conversation and every treatise. Everywhere, mosques, *madrasahs* (schools) and other public buildings were erected realizing the Arabesque in ever new forms, in marble, stucco, brick or paint. Everywhere, the aural Arabesque of the call of the *Mu'adhdhin* on the minarets to the faithful to rise for the ritual prayers punctuated the day of millions. During the month of Ramadan (fasting) the whole tempo of life changed following the timing and practices of the fast. When either of the two *ʿIds* came, only the largest open field of the district could hold the multitudes who came in their best and new clothing to kneel and prostrate themselves together in worship of the one transcendent God, in the beautiful Arabic verses of the Qur'an.

Cities sprang under the influence of Islam which were the model of town planning, utility, cleanliness and integration. Colleges and schools, public libraries, public baths, recreation areas and gardens, running water and draining systems, to make even our modern cities poor, if not hopeless, comparisons. And all this in the 9th and 10th centuries when Europe's cities, the heirs of classical antiquity could hardly boast of one paved street, or of one public night light other than the moon.

In the eleventh century, Muslim spirituality began to take a different turn. Prodded by an over enthusiastic love of God as expressed in Arabic poetry by the famous mystical poetess Rābiʿah al-ʿAdawiyyah, converts from Gnostic Christianity and Judaism, from Upanishadic Hindu mysticism and Buddhism, began to interpret Islam in mystical terms, shifting its emphasis from the actual where the divine will is to be concretized to the spiritual as such. The bridge which connected Islam to history, to space and time, and kept the Muslim's feet on the ground, snapped. Psychic and introspective analysis took the place of legal and juristic study. Alchemy, astrology and numerology slowly replaced chemistry, astronomy and mathematics. Even the social health of the Islamic family gave way to the withdrawing, resigning surrender of the mystical brotherhood. Engagement in the affairs of society and state so expressive of the Muslim's consciousness of vicegerency was slowly abandoned for contemplative bliss and mystical experience of the individualist and personalist. The state was left to whosoever desired to grab it, and the caliphs became the puppets of powerful but fissiparous army generals. When the gathering storm arrived in the Mongol (Tatar) invasion of Genghis Khan, the Muslim World fell like a ripe plum. One after another, its jewel cities were put to the torch, and its people to death or devastation.

The fire that followed spread in many directions, China, India, Russia and South West Asia. In the latter the tide was arrested at ʿAyn Jālūd in Palestine where Ibn Taymiyyah, the first and greatest Muslim reformer, managed to check the Mongol advance with an Egyptian army. In vain did he try many times earlier to awaken the Muslims to this peril. The forces of mysticism always defeated him and connived with the authorities against him. Despite his military success at ʿAyn Jālūd, Ibn Taymiyyah fell again to the intrigues of the Sufis (mystics) and died in jail in Damascus.

Ibn Taymiyyah's hard work and death, however, were not in vain. He produced a whole library, over 300 works, in which he diagnosed the Muslim disease on every front of life. The major villain was of course mysticism which succeeded in reorienting the Muslim away from history, from the world, from reason and common sense, and delivered him to introspective meditation. Sufism dulled his realism, drew him away from society, from his business, even from his family. Instead of his pursuit of the will of God as law, Sufism taught the Muslim to run after the impossible dream of union with God in gnosis or "mystical experience."

Ibn Taymiyyah's words were not heeded. And yet, the miracle happened. The Tatar hordes which brought the holocaust were Shamanists. In a generation or two, they were all converted to Islam, the religion and culture of the very peoples they vanquished. The conquerors settled *en masse* in Asia minor and, a generation later, they were ready to march again, this time under the banner of Islam. Still vibrant with the martial spirit with which they came from central Asia, the new converts to Islam now organized under the leadership of the house of ʿUthman (hence, the name "Ottoman"), pressed ever forward in the direction of Europe. The Byzantine and Russian Empires crumbled at their advance. Vienna was besieged by them until the last quarter of the seventeenth century. The Black and Caspian seas became Muslim lakes. Between Vienna and Constantinople (renamed Islampul, later corrupted to Istanbul) they planted many a Muslim community, many a Muslim city, and erected a new style of Islamic architecture on the foundations of the Byzantine.

It was only in the eighteenth century that their empire, the Ottoman Empire, began to decay from within for identically the same reasons which brought the downfall of the earlier Arab (ʿAbbāsī) Empire. It was also in the eighteenth century that the ideas of Ibn Taymiyyah revived, again mysteriously, in the very heart of Arabia, as yet untouched either by Ottoman decay or the West's ascendency. The reform movement was led by Muhammad ibn Abd al-Wahhab. Sufism was its *bete noire* against which it hurled its fury. On the positive side, the movement called itself "salafiyyah," that is, traditional. It had no object other than reestablishing the original vision of the fathers, before that vision was affected by Mysticism. Simultaneously or shortly afterwards, similar movements swept over the whole Muslim World. Western colonialism was then launched and the Muslim World fell again under alien dominion, was mercilessly fragmented and exploited, parts of it were settled by alien colonizers and their populations dispersed or were to be systematically destroyed.

Today colonialism is at an end; but not its vestiges, and influences. However, the Muslim peoples of the world are racing the clock to catch up with the rest of the world in economic and military power as well as in political awareness, unity and coordination. Their Islam remains the strongest ideology they ever knew, ready to move them again, and the world with them, if they but open their minds to its wisdom and their hearts to its appeal.